From Despair To Decision

LOUIS B. KRUPNICK, Ed.D. & ELIZABETH KRUPNICK

CompCare®
publications

A division of Comprehensive Care Corporation
2415 Annapolis Lane, Suite 140, Minneapolis, Minnesota 55441

Krupnick, Louis B., 1948—
    From despair to decision.

    1. Alcoholism.   2. Alcoholism—Treatment.
3. Alcoholism—Rehabilitation.   4. Alcoholics—Family
relationships.   5. Alcoholism and employment.
I. Krupnick, Elizabeth, 1949-   II Title.
HVO35.K78   1985   362.2′928   84-19868
ISBN 0-89638-081-5

Inquiries, orders and catalog requests should be addressed to:
CompCare Publications
2415 Annapolis Lane
Minneapolis, Minnesota 55441
Call toll free 800/328-3330
(Minnesota residents 612/559-4800)

Cover design by Jeremy Gale.
Cover art by Scott Baker.

To all chemically dependent families
for whom help is available.

Contents

Part two / Intervention: The technique

Part three / Intervention: The application

Foreword

Alcoholics and drug dependents get well only if they are confronted with a crisis so significant that it becomes suddenly less painful to give up the chemical than to continue using it. In the language of addiction and recovery, this crisis is called "hitting bottom," and it motivates a person to seek help.

Unfortunately, the level at which many alcoholic/ chemically dependent people hit bottom is too low to save them. By the time the motivating crisis comes, it is too late. Their bodies, minds, and spirits have been ravaged by a complex and devastating disease process.

The disease severely affects dependents' families too, who are inevitably caught in the tragic undertow. Friends, employers, and co-workers also may be affected, but these people, along with family members, are often frustrated in their attempts to help the dependent find relief from the stress, anxiety, depression, and deterioration which are part of the illness.

When health care or human service professionals without expertise in chemical dependency treatment try to help dependents and their families, the help frequently is as ineffectual as it is well-meant. Help which treats only the symptoms but not the disease protects dependents from the consequences of their chemical use, and the situation worsens.

Guided intervention is a technique which "raises the bottom" by inducing a crisis. Faced with this crisis, the chemically dependent person and the family can be propelled into a program of recovery. Interventions are not angry confrontations, encounter groups, or spontaneous uprisings. They are meetings, carefully and lovingly planned with the guidance of a specialist, of people close to the dependent. Thousands of interventions over the past fifteen years have demonstrated the effectiveness of the approach.

Guided interventions are successful for a variety of people with chemical problems. They are equally appropriate for a thirty-five-year-old business executive with a $2,000-a-week cocaine habit, a high-school-age beer drinker/marijuana smoker, a seventy-year-old retiree abusing prescription drugs, or a middle-aged alcoholic. Although there are wide pharmacological differences among mood-altering chemicals, the disruptions they cause in their victims' lives are more similar than different. So the term "chemical dependency" has emerged to describe the disease of all addicts, no matter what drugs are involved. Chemical dependency, of course, includes alcoholism.

Readers who are aware of the disease of chemical dependency but who are unfamiliar with the process of guided intervention may want to read Parts Two and Three (pages 55 and 83), Intervention: The Technique and Intervention: The Application. The descriptions of interventions will give readers a good understanding of the dynamics of an intervention.

We wrote an earlier edition of this book, *Rx Intervention: Something That Works,* designed for use with professional seminars led by Dr. Louis Krupnick, on the principles and practices of guided intervention. The present edition builds upon the first and includes answers to many of the questions raised in these seminars.

Pioneers in guided intervention techniques have contributed excellent books: Vernon Johnson (*I'll Quit Tomorrow*), Sharon Wegscheider (*Another Chance*), and Ruth Maxwell (*The Booze Battle*). We are grateful to these authors, to seminar participants, and to professional interventionists who reviewed their experiences with us.

We also learned a great deal from hundreds of patients and family members at the Alcoholism Recovery Center at Desert Hospital in Palm Springs, California, and at Eagle Hill Treatment Center in Sandy Hook, Connecticut, and from the many families who have begun their recovery through interventions.

Finally, and especially, we owe a large debt of thanks to Doris Krupnick, our mother, who is currently a counselor at Sierra Tucson, a chemical dependency treatment center in Tucson, Arizona. She has greatly increased our understanding of chemical dependency and the dynamics of recovery. Her experience and ideas are reflected throughout this book.

Louis B. Krupnick, Ed.D.
Elizabeth Krupnick
Hartford, Connecticut

Part one
Intervention: The background

1
Chemical dependency:
An equal opportunity disease

Sandra is a fifty-one-year-old housewife who has been taking Valium daily for more than four years. By her own admission, she "just can't get through a day without it."

Thomas doesn't call himself an alcoholic, but his heavy drinking has cost him his family, his home, and his law practice.

Nick, seventeen, a promising track athlete at a large suburban high school, has dropped out of school two months before graduation. Beer, wine, and marijuana have become more important to him than school, sports, his part-time job, even his girlfriend.

Despite the disruptions their addictions bring, Sandra, Thomas, and Nick cannot stop using drugs or alcohol. All three are truly dependent on these mood-altering chemicals.

Sandra, Thomas, and Nick, although they rely on different drugs, have much in common. Alcohol is, after all, a drug, and professionals in the addictions field have discovered that treatment and recovery processes are very similar for alcoholics and other drug dependents. The progression of the addiction and the accompanying family dysfunctions are, in general terms, the same whether the chemical is ethyl alcohol, cocaine, marijuana, prescription medications, or opiates. In this book, unless there are significant distinctions to be made among drugs and their effects, we will use the terms "chemical dependency" and "chemical dependents."

Is chemical dependency a disease, a personality disorder, or a character weakness? The question has been debated for two centuries. Over the years the most prevalent view has been that chemical dependency is the result of immorality or weakness of will. Consequently, for many years, an alcoholic or drug-dependent typically received little help beyond a disapproving warning to "pull yourself together."

Fortunately, the disease concept has been gaining acceptance since the mid-twentieth century. In 1951 the World Health Organization identified alcoholism as a complex disease process. Before the end of the 1950s, most major health organizations, including the American Medical Association, the American Psychiatric Association, and the American Public Health Association, recognized alcoholism as a disease. This perspective made it easier for the victim to admit the problem and encouraged the rapid development of a range of treatment services for the chemical dependent. During the 1960s, many insurance companies introduced coverage for the treatment of alcoholism/chemical dependency.

A 1982 Gallup poll showed that 79 percent of respondents agreed with the statement: "Alcoholism is a disease and should be treated as a disease in a hospital." (*Alcoholism Magazine*, February 1983). In the same survey, 59 percent of the respondents indicated that they believed "alcoholism treatment should be covered by medical insurance the same as any other disease." The discrepancy between the number of people who say they recognize alcoholism as a disease and the number who believe its treatment should be covered by insurance brings up an important point:

people still are ambivalent about the disease concept.

Alcoholism/chemical dependency meets the criteria of a disease. It has predictable symptoms. It is primary; that is, it is not caused by or secondary to another disease. It is progressive and chronic. If untreated, chemical dependency is fatal.

A primary disease

Chemical dependency is a primary disease. This means that chemically dependent persons must be treated for their dependency *before* other, related problems can be addressed. For example, there is little to be done for an alcoholic with pancreatitis until the drinking stops. Or sometimes, in the case of a drinking alcoholic who has been labeled a manic-depressive, the symptoms seem to lessen or vanish altogether after the person stops drinking.

Most treatment specialists also believe chemical dependency is primary; it *causes* rather than *is caused by* other health problems. So far, studies relating alcoholism and other drug dependencies to genetic or personality predispositions or chemical imbalances in the body have been inconclusive. In its simplest terms, alcohol is the cause of alcoholism, but what makes one out of ten drinkers alcoholic has researchers stumped. Fortunately, we do know that chemically dependent people can and do respond to treatment.

A progressive disease

Like many other illnesses, chemical dependency is

3

progressive. If untreated, it inevitably gets worse. Death can occur from severe disruption of organ functions, a general breakdown in the body's immune system, accidents, or suicide. The progressive nature of alcoholism has been described in detail by several authorities (Jellinek, 1960; Johnson, 1980; Wegscheider, 1981). In his book *I'll Quit Tomorrow,* an alcoholism classic, Dr. Vernon Johnson identifies four stages in the progression of alcoholism. These can be applied to other forms of chemical dependency.

The *learning* phase is experienced by everyone who takes a mood-altering substance for "recreational" or medical purposes. In this phase, a person is introduced to alcohol or another drug and the use is generally a pleasant experience.

Sam, for example, had his first couple of beers when he was fifteen. He enjoyed the relaxed feeling and giddiness. He learned that the beer made him "feel good."

Typically, in this first stage, a nice, friendly relationship is established between the person and the chemical. Sam, like most people, did not suffer negative consequences in the learning phase. Some are not so lucky, like the new drinker who has too many too fast and gets sick. But even this novice learns that with a little modification in consumption habits the drug will produce the desired effect the next time.

In the second stage, *seeking the mood swing,* the user is looking for the good feeling associated with using the drug. By the time Sam entered this phase, he had learned from his previous experience that the way to "feel really good" was to drink scotch for a while and then switch to beer. He believed he could drink more this way and not get "too loaded." Sometimes he would overdo it, especially at parties, but neither he nor others suffered significant consequences from his drinking.

As Sam slowly began to lose control of his drinking, he entered the third stage, *harmful dependency*. He would promise himself to "take it easy" by limiting his drinking to weekends and weekdays after work, but he rarely kept his promises. His alcohol use had notable consequences. A couple of his friends told him he was drinking too much, and his boss warned him about his long lunch breaks. Sam also started to worry about money. This was not surprising, because he was spending a lot of time — and money — in bars. Old friendships began to wane. People stopped inviting him to parties. Sam began to think that life, including his drinking, just wasn't as much fun as it once had been.

In the fourth stage, *using to feel normal*, Sam drank to ward off terrible anxiety and withdrawal symptoms. Yet when some of his friends confronted him with his drinking problem, he vehemently denied it and became abusive. Fired from his job, he explained to others that he resigned in order to start a business. Then, after a while, Sam could no longer remember whether he had resigned or had been fired, and it didn't seem to matter any more. His drinking became compulsive. His physical symptoms worsened to the point where they included frequent blackouts. He suffered deep and prolonged depressions and stopped seeing people altogether. At the age of twenty-five, Sam died in an automobile accident caused by his drinking.

While the rate of progression varies from person to person, the nature of the progression is remarkably similar whether the addiction is to prescription pills, illegal street drugs, or cocktails at the corner tavern.

A chronic disease

Chemical dependency is *chronic*. It is not merely a temporary condition like the flu. Since patterns of use vary deceptively, diagnosis is not always easy. For example, an alcoholic whose drinking is episodic — with weeks, months, or even years between binges — may appear to defy the chronic nature of the disease. Even so, the disease is only interrupted by "dry" periods. The symptoms and consequences continue to increase in severity when the person resumes drinking. One common saying is: "If you start drinking again, you begin where you left off." This is true with any addictive chemical.

Acceptance of chemical dependency as a disease has prompted many families and social service providers to seek help for alcoholics and other drug dependents. The past twenty years have brought an explosion in the number of hospital-based and free-standing treatment programs in the United States. Because appropriate treatment is now available, we no longer expect chemical dependents, as sick people, simply to "tough it out." The technique of guided intervention described in this book is often successful because it gives families, employers, and others a specific, practical way to help a person suffering from chemical dependency.

While the disease concept makes chemical dependency easier to identify and to treat, it causes some misunderstandings too. Some people assume that because chemical dependency is a disease, it can be "cured." There is confusion about the differences between chronic and acute diseases. Acute conditions such as appendicitis can be dealt with successfully once and for all. Scarlet fever and the measles run their one-time, miserable course and result in immunity against later attacks. But chronic diseases, such as diabetes and chemical dependency, cannot be cured. They can only be arrested, through proper care. There is no such thing as a "cured drug dependent" or an "ex-alcoholic" — only a recovering chemical dependent whose disease has been arrested.

The disease concept also may lead to a denial of responsibility for one's own recovery. Sometimes dependents hand over that responsibility to doctors or psychotherapists. Or they may say to themselves, "If there's no cure, why try?" A cocaine addict in treatment put it this way: "Whenever I relapsed, I figured, 'What the hell, if I've got a disease, I've got a disease. Why fight it?'"

The answer is: for an addict, life can be physically, emotionally, and spiritually healthier and infinitely more rewarding without the chemical.

2
The signs and symptoms of chemical dependency

Denial

Like other diseases, chemical dependency is character-ized by a unique set of symptoms. The most striking of these is *denial*, denial that the drug is being abused or is causing problems for the abuser and others. Denial may be manifested in several ways including minimization, rationalization, and projection. Many dependents exhibit all of these.

Dependents use *minimization* to deny the progres-sion of the disease to themselves and others. Examples:

- "I only have a couple of drinks in the evening." He doesn't mention that the drinks are doubles or that a "couple" really means three or four, and that the evening begins shortly after lunch.

- "I don't use sleeping pills very often, only when I have terrible insomnia." She doesn't acknowledge that her insomnia is a nightly problem.

- "Heroin isn't really a problem for me. I just chip on weekends." (Chipping means light, sporadic use.) The user doesn't say that the drug costs more each week than he earns in salary.

When dependents become uncomfortable with their alcohol or other drug use, they find reasons to *rational-ize* it. Examples of rationalization:

9

- "If you had to face the kind of pressure I get at work, you'd tip a few too."

- "My wife and I aren't getting along so well these days, so I guess I drink to keep myself from getting really angry at her. And I use coke because it helps me enjoy sex with her."

Projection is used to deny the reality of situations by blaming others. Whatever is emotionally unacceptable is attributed to someone else. An example of projection:

- "If you think I smoke a lot of dope, you should see my husband. He taught me how to smoke. If there's a problem, he's the one who has it!"

Blackouts and delusions

As chemical dependency progresses, defenses become more rigid and predictable. They are buttressed by another symptom of the disease, *sincere delusions.* These render dependents incapable of understanding the reality of their situations. Although chemically dependent persons are notorious for lying, they also may be truly unaware of events which have happened in the past or plans they have made for the future.

Delusions may be the result of chemically or psychologically induced *blackouts* or inaccurate recollections of behavior, called *faulty recall.* What initiates or stops a blackout is not understood. However, we do know that a *chemically induced* blackout produces amnesia lasting from a few minutes to a few weeks, or even longer. After the blackout has run its course, the dependent probably will not remember anything that took place during that period. The following is a typical conversation between a dependent and his wife after a blackout:

"Jack, why did you fly to New York after your business was finished in Boston?"

"What gave you that crazy idea?"

"Well, I just got the credit card bill and it has all sorts of entries for plane fares and two days at a hotel."

"It must be some kind of mistake. You know those credit card people are always messing up."

Jack doesn't remember being in New York, but he has an uneasy feeling that something is wrong.

Some blackouts are recalled to the extent that dependents know there is a period missing from their memories. Other blackouts are totally forgotten. In either case, blackouts understandably result in confusion, anger, fear, and feelings of craziness on the part of the dependent as well as family members and friends. The dependent takes refuge in defensive strategies such as social withdrawal, aggression, and other techniques to deflect concern away from the drinking or using behaviors. The dependent also may become paranoid. In response to blackouts, family members typically become isolated, depressed, angry, and overcome by feelings of powerlessness. The confusion resulting from blackouts is so great that some family members seek individual counseling for themselves in the belief that their own memories and perceptions are faulty ("I must be losing my mind").

Psychologically induced blackouts are all too successfully repressed memories — memories so painful that the dependent cannot accept them on a conscious level. Feelings of shame, guilt, and remorse about an incident build up to a point where the dependent simply forgets. These blackouts are not necessarily permanent; some therapies may unlock stored memories and make them accessible to the conscious mind. Of course, to an extent, we all repress uncomfortable and painful incidents in our lives, but in dependents this type of repression is more likely to be frequent and severe. Although some dependents never experience a blackout, the likelihood of blackouts increases as the disease progresses.

Faulty recall occurs when a dependent remembers a feeling associated with past behavior, but has an inaccurate recollection of the behavior. Faulty recall may be *euphoric.* For example, as far as Stan is concerned, yesterday's ball game was a whale of a good time. He remembers being witty and good-natured with his children. In reality, his son and daughter are so angry and ashamed about Stan's obnoxious behavior in the grandstand that they won't even talk to him.

Faulty recall also may be *apocalyptic.* A dependent's guilt, remorse, or other negative feeling is so entrenched that many recollections are tainted with self-hatred. For example, Juanita remembers people laughing at her at the company picnic. She assumes they were making fun of something stupid she must have said. Although this was not the case, Juanita will never know it. Her perceptions about herself are too distorted.

Growing preoccupation and other symptoms

A dependent's relationship to a chosen drug provides other symptoms: a growing preoccupation with the drug, self-medication, protection of supply, and changes in manner of use are important signs that the disease is progressing.

Dependents will structure their schedules around the drug use and avoid situations which would make it difficult to drink or to use. They also may talk about drugs at inappropriate times. The chemicals, seen as a panacea for all ailments and discomforts, become the dependents' best friends and lovers.

Addicts invariably want assurance of a ready supply of their drug. Protection of their supply generally leads to rationing, hoarding, or hiding bottles or pills around the house, car, office, or some other place. One creative alcoholic admitted in treatment that she had tucked an extra bottle of vodka in the cavity of a turkey which remained in her freezer for months. A teenager hid his stash of pot and pills in an air vent in the barn hay loft.

Besides worrying about supply, dependents typically lose interest in using their drug merely to be sociable. Now the goal of use is to get high — to avoid being sober. Other people may disturb the routine, so the dependent probably will begin to *use alone.*

Rapid use is another symptom of dependency. Chemically dependent people want quick results.

Many dependents use their drugs impulsively, without prior consideration. This *spontaneous use,* often totally inappropriate and illegal, can entail significant risk, as in the case of the high school sophomore who smoked marijuana in the girls' locker room, or of the stockbroker who snorted cocaine from the glass-topped desk in his office during business hours.

Another symptom of chemical dependency's progression is *growing tolerance.* As the disease progresses, dependents generally need more drugs or alcohol to reach the desired high. This growing tolerance is partially responsible for rapid intake, sneaking, and purchasing greater amounts. Ironically, increased tolerance is misinterpreted by many people as a sign that the victim is not dependent, since they see the dependent consuming large quantities without appearing to be high.

In the last stage of chemical dependency, especially alcoholism, dependents sometimes manifest *reverse tolerance.* Smaller amounts of the chemical are needed to achieve the desired effect and to ward off withdrawal symptoms. Although reverse tolerance is a clear sign of chemical dependency, many other signs will be manifested before this one. In fact, most alcoholics die without ever experiencing reverse tolerance. Unfortunately, dependents and their families often misinterpret this dangerous symptom as a sign of improvement.

Deterioration in several areas of life

Deterioration in relationships is a sign of dependency. Chemical dependents typically exhibit antisocial behavior resulting in a loss of old friendships, which they often replace with new relationships with other dependents, particularly those from a lower social or economic echelon. They usually curtail community and family activities. Dissolution of previously close family relationships may result in divorce, runaway children, and a high level of stress among family members.

Helping professionals, employers, and friends should be sensitive to the pain and symptoms of those close to the alcoholics, the co-dependents. Many counselors who are experienced in chemical dependency assessments believe co-dependents can be identified as easily as dependents. This topic is covered more fully in Chapter 3.

Deterioration in work performance can be a clue. The dependent is likely to become unreliable and unaccountably moody at work, but job performance does not always suffer noticeably. Many alcoholics and other drug abusers are able to appear normal on the job while their personal lives are crumbling. In spite of the dependent's effort to hold things together at work — and it often requires a supreme effort — co-workers and supervisors frequently sense when use of a chemical is becoming a problem.

In the same way, a chemically dependent student may show a drop in grades, sporadic class attendance, unreliability in meeting course requirements or keeping appointments. But teachers should be aware, too, that a seemingly "together" student, like the "normal on the job" dependent, may exhibit little change in performance, but still be in trouble with chemicals outside the school environment.

There is *spiritual deterioration* too. Personal values change as behavior violates standards the dependent once held. As the drug takes over the number one spot in the dependent's life, spiritual strengths and purpose decline. An outward manifestation is often decreased

15

involvement with religious institutions. A long-time church member may stop attending church altogether.

Physical symptoms

In addition to noticeable changes in behavior and attitudes, dependents also may exhibit a wide range of physical symptoms. Some of these are observable, while others cannot be detected without medical evaluation. These physical symptoms cannot be examined within the scope of this book, but it's important to dispel the notion that dependents will necessarily show serious physical deterioration, even in the latter stages of dependency. Some dependents appear healthy, while others exhibit dramatic symptoms. For example:

- In spite of her serious addiction to cocaine, Clara appeared healthy to her co-workers. In fact, they thought she had more zest than she once did. Outwardly, Clara held herself together well enough at work, but other areas of her life were falling apart. She developed hepatitis from using someone else's needle and, on the day she was given the Employee of the Month award, she collapsed in the elevator. Everyone with her at the time seemed to accept her explanation: "All this excitement must have made me a little dizzy."

- Larson's friends knew he was sick. So did his doctor. The friends knew because Larson's skin was yellow. His doctor knew because Larson's liver was so diseased that he had developed jaundice. He appeared much older than his sixty years. His face was puffy and his abdomen swollen. He suffered serious heartburn, alcoholic gastritis, and alternating diarrhea and constipation. His pulse was elevated. He was short of breath. He reported transient chest pain. His physician discovered that, since an examination six months earlier, Larson's blood pressure had risen dramatically. In addition, Larson reported vague pains and generalized weakness. Finally, Larson acted odd. His memory and concentration were impaired, and he seemed confused at times. He appeared very anxious; his bleary eyes darted around suspiciously.

Movies and television often portray alcoholics as sad-but-funny clowns or rumpled, down-and-out bumtown characters. Drug addicts are likely to be shown either as street people existing on the low fringe of society or as high rollers in Hollywood. These stereotypes are grossly inaccurate; they fail to depict over 95 percent of the dependent population. Alcoholics are decidedly not clowns. In fact, their lives are notably lacking in humor or joy. And very few chemically dependent persons will end up either on skid row or on the cover of *Rolling Stone*.

Social service and medical professionals must remember that chemical dependency is truly an equal opportunity disease. It spans all ages and social classes. It includes all races, nationalities, and religions. Males and females are equally vulnerable. Some dependents are street-wise opiate addicts, while others are hooked on prescribed tranquilizers. Some spend thousands of dollars a month on their chemical; others spend relatively little. Some lead a criminal life; others

17

never have legal problems. Some deteriorate visibly while others appear to be paragons of health. Some are mean; others are sweet. In short, anyone can be chemically dependent.

National figures on alcohol abuse indicate that one out of every eight drinkers will experience serious problems from drinking; and each dependent intimately affects an average of five or six other people. All mood-altering chemicals, whether they are considered physically addicting or not, have dangerous potentials for addiction. Chemical dependency is indeed an epidemic!

3
Chemical dependency
and the family

The problems of alcoholics and drug addicts are not suffered in isolation; virtually all chemically dependent people affect others — especially those closest to them. In fact, chemical dependency commonly is called a "family disease." Family members are dragged into a web of problems and symptoms with such predictability that the term *co-dependency* has been coined to describe the situation. Although no two families are precisely alike and no two families respond to chemical dependency in just the same way, there are some common themes, feelings, and roles which prevail in virtually all dependents' families.

Stages of the family disease

Just as the dependent suffers progressively greater consequences as a result of drinking or drug use, the family is affected in predictably progressive stages.

In the first stage, family members begin to experience anxiety about the dependent's use. While everyone in the family denies that the drinking or drug problem exists, family relationships become more strained. There are arguments, there is tension, and people do not communicate what they really believe or feel.

During the second stage, the whole family becomes preoccupied with the dependent's chemical use. Family members have sincere delusions about the reality of the disease. At the same time, they attempt to control the pattern of use and the consequences of abuse. Family life becomes increasingly unmanageable as members develop physical and emotional symptoms and often pull back from social involvement outside the home. An implicit or explict agreement, known as the "no talk" rule, goes into effect: family members don't discuss alcohol or other drug use in any way which could threaten their delusion that "Chemical use is not causing any problems in *this* family; we're handling it just fine without any help from anybody."

In the third stage, family members assume rigid and predictable roles. They become "enablers" (described on page 22) and severely dysfunctional. In this stage, denial of emotional pain and other feelings is common.

During the fourth stage, major family crises are likely to occur. As weary family members seek ways to escape from their untenable situation, there may be complete emotional disengagement or divorce — even suicide or homicide. At the same time, the family unit is likely to continue to have strong, protective feelings toward the dependent. The fourth stage is perhaps best characterized by emotional exhaustion.

Feelings

As the disease progresses, family members experience a range of feelings. These include:

- *Anger:* Anger toward the dependent's behavior may become generalized to the point where co-dependents frequently or usually appear angry.

- *Resentment:* Co-dependents understandably resent the bizarre behavior, broken promises, and dishonesty which characterize chemically dependent people.

- *Pain:* It is painful to watch — and to be part of — the disintegration of an individual and a family.

- *Shame:* Co-dependents are ashamed of the dependent's embarrassing behavior. This humiliation may grow into shameful feelings about themselves, particularly as the disastrous consequences of use demonstrate the increasing powerlessness of everyone in the family.

- *Guilt:* Family members blame themselves and each other for episodes of problem use. Children especially feel guilty about "causing" problems. "If I got better grades (made the team, turned down my stereo) maybe Mom wouldn't drink."

- *Loneliness:* Co-dependents feel isolated from each other and from people outside the family.

- *Fear:* Co-dependents fear the future, the unknown, accidents, arguments, violence, and financial ruin. Even weekends, parties, and family gatherings provoke anxiety.

- *Feeling out of touch:* As the disease progresses, family members become increasingly unable to experience feelings of love or concern for the dependent, others in the family, and themselves. As healthy communication breaks down, they become emotionally estranged and live a lie based on delusions.

Enabling

Enabling is any behavior which, however well-intentioned, serves to protect dependents from the consequences of their use, thereby contributing to a worsening of the disease in dependents and co-dependents. Some examples of enabling behaviors:

• *Denying* that the drinking or drug use constitutes a primary problem.

Despite overwhelming evidence that her husband had started drinking again, Ellen maintained to her friends, and to herself, that everything was okay. Even when he came home drunk, Ellen accepted his explanation that he had been given too much medication at the dentist's office.

• *Avoiding* problems and conflicts which might "cause" the dependent to use alcohol or drugs.

Frank's business ran into difficulty because of an unexpected shortage of raw materials. He and Nancy had planned to go on an expensive vacation, and he decided not to cancel it because he feared Nancy would go off on a bender. They took the trip, then came home to find the business in even worse shape. Nancy went on a binge over *that*.

• *Minimizing* the problems associated with the dependent's chemical use or the amount used.

Pearl's parents were upset at the high school principal when he called to tell them that Pearl was being suspended. She had been caught giving a small quantity of pot to another student. Her parents believed that other problems were a lot worse than pot-smoking, and they figured that if the other girl, a seventh grader, wanted to smoke marijuana, Pearl could hardly be considered a criminal for letting her have some.

• *Rationalizing* the use by excusing the dependent's increasingly inappropriate behavior as due to other causes.

When Louisa started to use tranquilizers, her husband Juan assumed she would need them only temporarily. After two-and-a-half years she was taking progressively larger doses. Juan was concerned about Louisa's tranquilizer use, but he reassured himself that her doctor probably knew best.

• *Protecting* the dependent from the natural and logical consequences of chemical use.

Margaret knew that her boss was apt to make impulsive decisions, forget what he'd said, and fly off the handle after his long lunches, so she scheduled his important appointments for the morning.

• *Controlling* people and situations in order to control chemical use; trying to control the amount of alcohol or other drug consumed.

The cost of Max's cocaine habit had risen to $500 a week when his girlfriend, Marilyn, decided to do something about it. Max did not want to stop using, so Marilyn resorted to some manipulative measures. She insisted that Max join her on weekend junkets to the country, hoping that he would slow down his use if he didn't do so much partying. When that didn't work, she mixed lactose powder into his cocaine and then stole half his stash. Max started buying greater quantities of coke, vaguely planning to sell some but snorting all of it.

• *Waiting and hoping* that "things will get better — just be patient."

After reassigning him twice to less stressful jobs, Harrison's employer finally forced him to take early retirement. His family had hoped the transfers would help him cut down on his drinking, but, in fact, the drinking got worse. They hoped he would relax and drink less when he retired. He didn't. Although his disease was progressing rapidly, they continued to wait, hoping that he would "get used to retirement." Harrison continued to drink until he died of kidney failure.

• *Living by the "no talk" rule* about chemical use creates other taboo subjects, too, including family finances, sex, and family relations. Personal feelings, attitudes, values, and fears, especially in any context which would threaten the shaky balance of the family, also are forbidden topics.

Steve was an attorney in a small community. His wife, Susan, thought he drank too much but was afraid to say so. Besides, she didn't want the children to know their father had a drinking problem, so she didn't talk with them about it and forbade them to mention it. Susan worried constantly that Steve's associates and clients would find out about his problem. She also worried about her sexual relationship with Steve. They had talked about it a little, but not openly. After Susan tried to tell him that she didn't like making love when he was drunk, Steve acted depressed for a week. Susan never brought up the issue again until she was introduced to the concept of guided intervention. During family counseling sessions at the center Steve finally went to for treatment, family members were "allowed" to talk about their worries and concerns. They also learned to express their love for each other.

The "no talk" rule is pervasive in chemically dependent families and epitomizes their predictable denial. Until the "no talk" rule can be punctured, there is little realistic hope of recovery for the family.

Although many others outside the family unwittingly contribute to the progression of a dependent's disease through enabling behaviors, what distinguishes co-dependents from other enablers is obsession. Co-dependents' very existence — like the victim's — revolves around the drug. They constantly attempt to control the dependent's use of the drug — and their own behavior — so the dependent won't embarrass them or suffer significant consequences. This constitutes a full-time job!

Adaptive roles

Specialists in the treatment of chemically dependent families, and the families themselves, have come to recognize that there are some predictable ways in which family members adapt to the problem of chemical dependency. This fact in no way negates or belittles the unique pain each family member suffers.

The following material is based in large part on the

work of Sharon Wegscheider, who credits the concept of family roles in a crisis to earlier work by Virginia Satir.

In a family struggling to cope with alcoholism or drug addiction, individuals adjust to the situation through adaptation. Because the problem is chronic and progressive, there is tremendous motivation for each member to figure out a way to maintain emotional equilibrium. This goal is almost impossible to achieve as long as the problem drug use continues, but each co-dependent tries to survive emotionally by taking on a certain family role — or sometimes more than one role at a time.

Sharon Wegscheider identifies five specific roles which co-dependents may assume in their effort to adapt to a situation which has become emotionally unbearable. Don Wegscheider in his book *If Only My Family Understood Me* and Claudia Black in her book *It Will Never Happen to Me* also have described similar roles — with different labels — in chemically dependent families. The roles, according to Sharon Wegscheider, are these:

Chief Enabler

The Chief Enabler, often the spouse, is the person closest to and most relied upon by the dependent. The Chief Enabler's feelings are repressed anger, worry, and resentment. While apt to be judgmental, the Chief Enabler also is laden with guilt and plagued by the delusion that there might be something more he or she should do or should have done for the dependent. The Chief Enabler often:

- Becomes overly responsible in order to handle the dependent's obligations.

- Protects the dependent from the consequences of chemical use, thereby delaying a crisis that could lead to recovery.

- Attempts to manipulate people and to control situations in order to remove any possible reason for the dependent to use liquor or other chemicals.

- Struggles to make life manageable for the entire family.

- Becomes a chronic worrier.

- Is deluded about the reality of his or her own situation and accepts the projections of the dependent. Takes on the blame for "causing" the chemical problems.

- Neglects self. Nutrition and exercise are ignored. Emotional and sexual needs go unfulfilled.

- Suffers stress-related physical symptoms, such as headaches, gastrointestinal problems, nervousness, and back pain.

- Withdraws from social activities both because the dependent's behavior is increasingly antisocial and because the demands placed on the Chief Enabler don't leave much time or energy for socializing.

- Suffers decreased effectiveness in job responsibilities and is likely to miss work.

- Is in danger of prescription-pill dependency or alcoholism. May start to abuse drugs in an attempt to make the dependent's use more manageable. ("If I have a few drinks with him, maybe he'll stop at a few." Or "Maybe if she sees what cocaine does to me, she'll stop using it herself.")

- Has a high probability, if divorced from this dependent, of marrying another chemically dependent person.

The Chief Enabler is the most likely person in the family to initiate an intervention. This is true not only because of that person's habitual super-responsibility, but also because the Chief Enabler is the one who has most consistently tried — and failed — to help the dependent in other ways.

Family Hero

The Family Hero, according to Sharon Wegscheider, is usually the oldest child. The Hero's inability to help the dependent brings on feelings of inadequacy and guilt. The Hero places absurd expectations on self and others, and feels angry when these expectations are not met. However, the anger is denied and repressed because it is unacceptable to the Family Hero's concept of herself/himself. The Family Hero:

- Learns that the best way to stay out of trouble with the dependent or the Chief Enabler is to be perfect and to look for ways to give people what they want.

- Attempts to help the family in order to help herself or himself, but the pathology of the family thwarts this goal.

- Becomes a good student and is likely to excel in sports, music, or other school activities.

- Is seen by people outside the family as a successful person. The Hero fosters a sense of family worth.

- Denies the existence of negative feelings.

- Learns and enforces the "no talk" rule.

- Overextends and develops psychosomatic symptoms common to workaholics — migraines, ulcers, and circulatory diseases.

- Becomes hypercritical and judgmental, wanting others to try harder to make things better.

- Prefers admiration and respect to intimacy and love.

- Is often resistant to family treatment because of a carefully constructed facade of strength.

- May become the Chief Enabler in a new family.

- Is likely to enter social service professions or assume supervisory roles in chosen work; is more comfortable leading than following.

Scapegoat

The Scapegoat, often the second child, is usually angry at parents, the world, and self. The anger masks the more painful feelings of being an outcast. Guilt and shame are common feelings for this child. The Scapegoat:

- Withdraws from the family by running away, rejecting family values and norms. The Scapegoat may seek escape through chemical use.

- Diverts attention from the family's primary issue of chemical dependency by manifesting aberrant and antisocial behavior.

- Fights for recognition in whatever way possible.

- Often has behavior problems in school and may get into trouble with the law.

- Attempts to find the intimacy and self-worth lacking in the family. Female Scapegoats are likely to become pregnant during their teens.

- Feigns an uncaring attitude.

- Is a high suicide risk.

- May exploit friends and others to get results.

- Is very sensitive; may learn to help others in distress if treatment is received.

Scapegoat behavior may create a crisis which knowledgeable professionals can use to assess the family for chemical dependency.

Lost Child

The Lost Child, often the family's third child, withdraws from the family and becomes a loner. This child feels worthless and no one bothers to contradict this perception. The Lost Child:

- Is passive and expects little from self or others.

- Has difficulty developing intimate relationships with others.

- Has trouble making choices and commitments, "goes along to get along."

- Is likely to be ineffectual but gets by because he or she doesn't cause trouble.

- May actually provide some relief from the tensions in the family, because this dreamy one can be counted on not to make waves — or even ripples ("no news is good news"). Helps to maintain the illusion of normalcy.

- Is likely to have overweight or illness problems, which offer ways of receiving attention without having to ask for it.

The Lost Child actually has a good potential for recovery if he or she joins Alateen (or Al-Anon as an

31

adult child of a dependent). Recovery is based on the development of sensitivity, assertiveness, and self-reliance.

Family Mascot

The Family Mascot is likely to be the youngest child or the youngest girl. The Mascot's self-esteem is based on the ability to satisfy other people's need for diversion. As the family clown, she or he attempts to bring some humor to a family overwhelmed by unspoken pain. The Mascot:

- Acts fidgety, helpless, and immature.

- Has difficulty establishing her own priorities and commitments.

- Maintains family rituals that provide structure for good times.

- Is not taken seriously and learns not to take herself (or himself) seriously, but continues to demand attention. May be hyperactive.

- Is likely to be intelligent and resourceful, but limited in ability to concentrate. Breadth of responsiveness and depth of understanding are stunted.

- Will find it hard to grow up and develop relationships based on mutuality. Is likely to be manipulative and domineering in future relationships.

- Has a high probability of becoming addicted to prescription pills.

- Has hope for recovery if she or he can develop the confidence that another life stance is possible, emotionally safe, and potentially more satisfying.

When a family resists

Clearly, chemically dependent families suffer from many problems. They develop rigid roles to cope with stress that is never openly discussed. They live in fear of the future. They suffer from denial of reality and the consequences of self-defeating enabling behaviors.

Despite their desire to see the dependent stop abusing chemicals, they actually contribute to the pile-up of problems. They feel ashamed, not only of the chemically dependent members but of themselves. They have hidden the truth for so long that they find it hard to confront their own feelings.

It's not surprising that many families resist outside efforts to intervene. They probably have tried and failed many times to improve their situation and may be terrified by the idea of breaking through the familiar wall that has imprisoned them.

Many co-dependents, when they initially hear about guided interventions, object to participating because they believe they would be "betraying" or "turning in" the dependent. Such a guilt reaction is understandable for co-dependents who have been so protective.

Chemically dependent families require patient help from experienced professionals in order to develop the desire, confidence, and ability to intervene in their loved ones' disease. But before preparing families for interventions, helping professionals need to address some of their own enabling behaviors which can make them ineffective in their work.

4
Professional enablers

Health and human service professionals frequently are frustrated in their attempts to be of real service to chemically dependent persons and their families. These families' dysfunctions trap them; members are seldom able to communicate the reality of their situation to each other, let alone to a physician, minister, or psychotherapist. They often cover up their feelings. They sometimes lie. They may not follow treatment plans even when they helped establish them.

In short, dependents and co-dependents are difficult clients. But there are ways for professional helpers to work with them effectively — if they have specialized training in chemical dependency, and if they have sorted out their own feelings about the disease. Like a lot of other people, these helpers often have not developed attitudes about chemical dependency which provide a good basis for understanding and helping.

The concept of enabling applies to professionals as well as to families and friends. Professional enablers include the physician who tells a patient, "Sam, you'd better slow down a bit on your drinking. You're not as young as you once were." Or the therapist who, week after week, allows her client to postpone exploring his drug use because she wants him to be the leader in their work together. Professionals who wait for victims deluded by alcoholism or drug abuse to "hit bottom" are enablers too.

Problems common to most helping professionals who work with dependents and their families include:

- A lack of knowledge about chemical dependency and the dynamics of recovery. Many professionals have the mistaken belief that dependents could stop using if they really wanted to.

- Resentment at being conned or manipulated. A chemical dependent is a master manipulator. This may cause the helping professional to withdraw emotionally from the dependent.

- A feeling of powerlessness, making it impossible to confront the dependent effectively.

- A fear of professional inadequacy, which may lead to an avoidance reaction.

- A professional "no talk" rule associated with politeness, confidentiality, and uneasiness — even a fear of legal retaliation from the dependent or family member.

- Denial of or discomfort with one's own chemical use or use by a member of one's family (even if that person is now sober and straight, or dead).

These problems essentially are restatements of issues affecting dependents' families and friends. However, the nature of helping relationships results in a special kind of stress on professionals, for helpers are supposed to *help*. This expectation is the foundation upon which the relationship is built. When the help is ineffective, disappointment sets in. Eventually a sense of futility engulfs both the client and the professional.

There is a widespread assumption that people must be motivated to change before change is possible; professionals are taught to help people who *want* help. So they wait for clients to tell them what's wrong and ask for help. This is often unrealistic with alcoholics and other drug-dependents because they genuinely may not know what is wrong. Or, if they do, they typically try to hide the truth. Here is one woman's story:

During my thirty-five years of alcoholic drinking that followed a classic, progressive course, I was enabled by many people. But the authority of physicians was especially forceful in condoning my drinking and, in some cases, thwarting my own tentative breaks in denial.

By the time I was thirty-seven, I was drinking heavily and experiencing blatant symptoms of alcoholism. After an especially violent argument, my husband left on a business trip. I started drinking and couldn't sleep. The family doctor came to the house, gave me an injection to sleep and a prescription for Seconal to be taken every four hours. He made no comment about the alcohol on my breath, my slurred speech, or my stumbling. This episode was followed by acute anxiety, depression, and aching jaws. After a few more incidents and injections for sleep, the doctor referred me to a psychiatrist. I saw this doctor twice weekly, on Tuesday mornings and Fridays after dinner. The Friday appointments were far more emotional and "productive" than the Tuesday sessions, and the doctor observed that I was more "accessible" in the evening after I had been through the dinner cocktail-and-wine ritual. I knew that he was disappointed in my "morning resistance," so I compensated by stopping for a brandy and Benedictine before each Tuesday appointment. There must have been heavy alcohol fumes in that little office, but they were never mentioned.

I finally told this psychiatrist that I thought perhaps I drank too much and that my husband was, at times, distressed about my behavior when I drank. The doctor asked me how much I drank, and I reported half the true amount. He made a mathematical computation using my weight and age and gave me the happy news that there was no problem. But apparently he had some residual concern because he later prescribed Librium, which at that time was viewed as an acceptable substitute for heavy drinking and a means of relief for the tension that caused my jaws to ache. I continued with the Seconal and alcohol as well as the Librium. After about eighteen months I discontinued treatment — but not the alcohol or pills.

I moved to another city, and the drinking became more and more out of control. I saw a counselor at the local chapter of the National Council on Alcoholism. We quickly agreed that I was, indeed, an alcoholic. She referred me to a physician who specialized in alcoholism treatment. I saw this specialist several times. She prescribed Antabuse, arranged for an AA contact, and referred me to a psychiatrist who specialized in addictions. I talked this over with my internist who said I wasn't the alcoholic "type." He smiled at me rather indulgently, and neither of us ever spoke of it again. He did, however, suggest amphetamines for low blood pressure and weight control. I took Dexedrine for several years.

The psychiatrist referred by the National Council on Alcoholism chapter was a man of great integrity, and I found it a relief to be able to talk to him about my drinking. We did much good work together. During this period I ceased daily drinking and instead went on one-

or two-day binges every few months. After a binge, we explored the emotional state that had led up to it. I saw that my drinking was a response to situations that tapped into early emotional deprivations, and viewed myself as a hapless victim.

After two years of orthopedic problems and several surgeries, I was not only addicted to alcohol, but also tranquilizers, sleeping pills, and pain medication. When I moved again, I panicked that I wouldn't be able to get the pills I needed, but within days I located a physician who kept me supplied for several months. During this period of progressively heavier use of these drugs, my family confronted me about my slurring speech and mental lethargy. In response, I consumed a quart of vodka along with an indeterminate amount of pills and was unconscious for several hours.

At age fifty-five, I entered treatment for alcoholism, still denying any addiction to drugs. I held to that belief until the withdrawal began. Only then did I accept that I was addicted to all mind- and mood-altering drugs.

After I returned home from the treatment center, I saw the doctor who had been so cooperative in ordering refills and told him how I had been manipulating him and offered an apology. He said he had known all along what was going on but believed I was a strong woman and could handle the situation. When I visited my old treatment center a year later, I found that doctor registered as a patient for chemical dependency.

Physician enabler

Medical doctors and other health care professionals may enable the progression of their patients' chemical dependency by:

- Failing to get a reliable history of chemical use from each patient and/or spouse.

- Not learning enough about chemical dependency to recognize it as a primary, progressive, chronic, and treatable disease.

- Succumbing to dependents' manipulative behaviors and verbal assaults.

- Failing to communicate an honest diagnosis and prognosis to patients.

- Prescribing mood-altering drugs.

- Failing to request case consultations from chemical dependency specialists. (This stems from the sad fact that many health professionals do little more than pay lip service to the disease concept of chemical dependency. It would be rare to see similar resistance to consultation with specialists for other health problems.)

- Waiting and hoping. "Perhaps she will pull herself together."

Physicians skilled at assessing chemical dependency can be of great help to their patients. In order to avoid enabling, physicians and others in health care should:

- Educate themselves about the signs and symptoms of chemical dependency.

- Ask patients if they are concerned about their own or a family member's chemical use. If they identify a problem, encourage them to talk with someone from AA or a treatment program.

- Ask patients and their spouses to respond to the questionnaire on page 111. Discuss their answers with them and assess whether they are responding honestly and whether there is a problem. Express concerns directly to the patient and spouse.

- Learn about treatment resources in their area. Develop relationships with chemical dependency specialists and use them for consultations and evaluations as appropriate.

- Follow up assessments or formal diagnoses with specific recommendations. If necessary, ultimatums can be used. For example, a physician might tell his patient, "Mr. Kline, I am concerned about your pancreas, and about your drinking. From my experience and examination, I think you will die within six months to a year unless you receive treatment. Treatment for your pancreas is not possible unless you stop drinking. I cannot in good faith continue as your doctor unless you stop drinking. However, I believe you may be able to recover your health with specialized care which I cannot provide. I have scheduled you and Mrs. Kline for an appointment with Dr. Symington who is a specialist in this field. Will you see him this afternoon?"

- Explain that chemical dependency is a disease. Patients may be more willing to accept the need for treatment if they know that for more than twenty-five years the AMA, the World Health Organization, and other major health organizations have recognized chemical dependency as a treatable disease, and that many insurance companies cover treatment.

Psychotherapist enabler

Many dependents and co-dependents seek help from psychotherapists. Unfortunately, the potential for professional enabling is very high among psychologists, psychiatrists, social workers, mental health counselors, and family therapists. Some of the reasons for this are the same as they are for other helping professionals, and some are unique to the counseling field.

One serious problem is a lack of accurate knowledge about chemical dependency. This is evident from the sections on "Alcohol Abuse" and "Alcohol Dependence" in the *Diagnostic and Statistical Manual of Mental Disorders* (*DSM III*), the diagnostic bible of the counseling profession.

The criteria used to distinguish abuse from dependency in *DSM III* are so hazy that professional diagnoses frequently support dependents' natural tendency to minimize. Counselors using the manual might logically diagnose a late stage dependent as a "mere" abuser. This contributes to the widespread professional delusion that terribly disruptive and prolonged abuse does not constitute dependence. As a consequence, too many therapists enable dependency in their clients by misdiagnosing and mistreating the problem. This is especially true because it is difficult to get reliable information from alcoholic or drug-dependent clients. A therapist may be lucky to have a client who discusses his or her symptoms of withdrawal and increased tolerance, but this would be rare. Dependents generally try to hide their symptoms as part of an elaborate system of defenses. Unfortunately, the *DSM III* does not even address the issue of dependents' delusions and denial of reality.

Other problems common to psychotherapists include:

- Confusion about the primacy of chemical dependency and reluctance to deal with it as a disease rather than as a problem of will power.

- Failure to get an accurate history of chemical use from the client or spouse.

- Mistaken belief that insight will lead the client to a sensible pattern of use.

- Belief that the client should lead the way in therapy; lack of understanding about denial, sincere delusions, blackouts, and other characteristics of dependents — as well as about family symptoms.

- Unfortunate willingness to stick with chemically dependent clients as long as they will keep coming and paying for therapy.

- Reliance on individual treatment. One-to-one counseling is a long-shot method of treatment unless combined with group therapy and/or attendance at AA or NA (Narcotics Anonymous) meetings. The support and confrontation that characterizes groups is generally more effective for dependents than individual work. A group of chemically dependent peers is less likely to be conned by a dependent's manipulations.

- Relying *solely* on family therapy. As Sharon Wegscheider in her book *Another Chance* explained the danger, the counselor "may soon be taking responsibility for the Dependent, sympathizing with the Enabler, admiring the Hero, rejecting the Scapegoat, ignoring the Lost Child, and failing to take the Mascot seriously — just like 'one of the family.' " The therapist who becomes part of the "family trap," as Wegscheider calls it, will be virtually unable to facilitate useful growth.

In order to treat dependents successfully, therapists must have education and training for working with this special group. They should also:

- Attend AA and NA meetings and familiarize themselves with the Twelve Steps (see page 109).

- Be willing to refer clients to interventionists and treatment programs.

- Meet with family members to aid in assessment if there is a concern that a client may be dependent.

- Terminate counseling treatment if it appears to be ineffective and enabling rather than productive. When this is necessary, the client should be fully informed of the reasons for termination and should be given a clear assessment and prognosis — as well as a recommendation for places or persons to go to for help.

Enabling by pastoral counselors

Religious institutions probably have more regular contact with entire families than any other institutions or agencies in this country, yet clergy account for a very small percentage of referrals to chemical dependency treatment centers.

Clergy suffer from the same lack of education about chemical dependency as other helpers. They often lack the awareness and knowledge to make an accurate assessment of dependency or co-dependency. Even when priests, ministers, and rabbis are aware of a dependency problem in one of their families, they may unwittingly enable its progression by:

- Dealing with it as a moral issue and relying exclusively on prayer to solve the problem. Clergy frequently refer to scripture and exhort families to pray for improvement. A good adage for pastoral counselors is "pray for a good harvest, but keep on hoeing."

- Stressing the role of will power to control addictions.

- Confusing being "nice" with being supportive or

45

helpful. Clergy, like other professionals, need to be able to confront painful and embarrassing situations. Because of the stigma commonly associated with alcoholism and other drug dependencies, there usually is a curtain of secrecy which shrouds afflicted families. Religious leaders must be prepared to open this curtain so that effective treatment can be pursued.

Here are some ways religious leaders can help chemical dependents and their families:

- They can develop evaluation skills and make the commitment to use them. This frequently will lead to calling in a specialist or organizing a guided intervention.

- They should convey that chemical dependency is a treatable family illness with certain predictable symptoms and well-established procedures for recovery.

- They should project an acceptance of the disease and express confidence that it can be treated.

- They can become knowledgeable about the Twelve Step program as a path to recovery and promote AA, NA, and Al-Anon meetings in their church rooms.

- They can help recovering clients grow spiritually.

Enabling by employers

Chemically dependent persons rarely leave their disease at home: they carry it with them wherever they go, including the workplace. So employers should be concerned about the effects of chemical dependency.

All too often, employers, managers, and supervisors unwittingly enable dependents to continue destructive drinking or drug use. The employer who assumes that "it's none of my business" may stand by and watch as valuable human resources — and profits — are lost. In fact, it is a matter of good business to provide assistance to chemically dependent employees. Alcoholism and other drug addictions impair job performance and lower productivity in any organization. In most cases, providing assistance to a chemically dependent employee is very cost-effective when the expense of replacing the employee and training a new one is calculated.

Examples of enabling by employers and managers:

- Overlooking aberrant behavior, lateness, sloppy work, long lunches, and other possible symptoms.

- Assuming dependents' responsibilities to lighten their load.

- Avoiding confrontation.

- Waiting and hoping for change.

- Subtly or directly telling employees that alcoholism/chemical dependency is automatic grounds for dismissal. As we have said, will power alone does not lead to recovery. If employees are not reassured that their jobs will be waiting for them when they complete a treatment program, they are less likely to accept the need for treatment.

• Failing to offer any type of Employee Assistance Program (EAP).

EAPs can be formal programs in large organizations or informal policies in smaller companies. In either case it is important for employers to:

• Recognize that alcoholism and drug abuse impair performance and entail great suffering for dependents and their families. Employers also should recognize that dependents' problems adversely affect other employees.

• Confront dependent employees and offer support for appropriate treatment. They should notify the employees' spouses or other family members about the situation and try to involve them in the assessment, referral, or intervention process.

• Take disciplinary measures, when necessary, to compel the chemically dependent employee to recognize the problem.

• Provide appropriate training and institutional support to supervisors who are responsible for implementing EAP policy. Unless these people are motivated and feel support from above, policies remain on paper.

• Prevent management and unions from developing tensions over EAP policies and procedures.

Dependents sometimes play union against management to protect themselves against dealing with their problem.

- Make certain that EAPs are appropriately designed to help all levels of employees, from executives to those on the lowest pay scale.

Employers can be powerful interventionists because of their generally perceived right to expect a certain level of job performance. This right to intervene is viewed as more legitimate than that of friends, doctors, counselors, or ministers. Only families and the legal system are seen as having similar rights to induce a dependent to accept treatment. Employers have great leverage with employees — the job!

EAP personnel also can be invaluable to recovering employees by making appropriate referrals to aftercare support groups and by helping with financial and vocational planning or other problems that may affect recovery and job performance. They can be useful, too, in recommending to management adjustments in the employee's work assignments to allow for less stress on the job, or time for outpatient treatment, AA meetings, and other elements in a recovery program.

The role of schools

Any effort to help alcoholics and drug abusers in schools must start with a commitment from the school board and the superintendent's office to establish an organized, comprehensive program, including an EAP. Some administrators may not see the connection between alcohol or other drug problems among staff and similar problems among students, but every school system has teachers and staff members who are recognized by their colleagues and students as alcohol or drug abusers. Students and the community must see that schools are "taking care of their own" before they will be responsive to a program to help students.

American parents are reeling at the climbing rates of alcohol and other drug dependencies among children and adolescents. Administrators, counselors, and teachers should be trained to recognize the symptoms, to communicate their concerns to parents, and to ask for evaluations by youth chemical dependency professionals. On the strength of these professional evaluations, schools should make referrals to appropriate treatment facilities and support groups for recovering students.

Teachers need to be aware of their own enabling behaviors. Most teacher-enabling happens through lack of awareness — or fear of "opening up a can of worms." It is unfortunate that most teachers are ill-equipped to deal with alcoholic and drug-addicted youth, because teachers often are in an excellent position to recognize the problems and to urge young people to seek help. They may see the signs of dependency in the classroom, on the playground, or at the lunch table. Although no teacher can be expected to serve as doctor-therapist-counselor-parent, teachers should, at a minimum:

- Be educated to recognize the most basic and obvious signs of drug and alcohol abuse.

- Acknowledge to drug-abusing students and their families an awareness of the young person's drug use and recommend a professional evaluation.

- Work with parents, friends, school counselors, other teachers, and youth chemical dependency experts in the community to intervene.

- Have current information on appropriate resources in the community in order to make effective referrals.

The role of attorneys and law enforcement officials

As they lose control over their drug use and their lives, dependents are likely to get in trouble with the law. This increases their chances of becoming involved with the legal system — public safety officers, attorneys, and judges.

Attorneys, like physicians, enjoy a reputation that makes them powerful. They have specialized knowledge, are well educated and generally articulate. They serve as a buffer between individuals and serious trouble. For these reasons, attorneys are in a particularly good position to question dependents and their families about difficulties resulting from chemical use. Attorneys can help rather than enable by:

- Insisting that someone, usually the spouse, join the initial consultation when the legal issue is likely to relate to chemical use.

- Using the questionnaire on page 111.

- Being prepared to make informed referrals to interventionists or treatment specialists. Attorneys should have release-of-information forms completed so they can legally talk with other professionals, including a client's physician and an interventionist.

An enlightened judge who mandates a year's attendance in AA or treatment for a DWI offender may have made a lifesaving decision for an alcoholic, the family, and other drivers.

When law enforcement personnel and other professionals in the legal system deal with people who are in trouble as a result of chemical dependency, they also can be helpful by:

- Taking action when a driver is clearly under the influence of a mood-altering chemical, first to get the driver off the road and into a detoxification program.

- Avoiding plea-bargaining procedures which permit drunk and chemically affected drivers (even second and third offenders) to keep their licenses and get light sentences.

- Prohibiting citizens whose driving licenses have been suspended for DWI from operating boats and aircraft.

- Making referrals to treatment programs instead of alcohol information schools, and recommending formal evaluations if there is a possibility that the offender may be dependent.

Police and public safety departments should provide training for all of their officers and reserve officers in the disease of chemical dependency.

Part two
Intervention: The technique

5
Guided intervention:
The technique

Guided intervention is not an isolated event. It is a process involving many stages. The actual, scheduled intervention will be most successful if there is careful planning and effective follow-up. But before any other steps can be taken, a thorough assessment must be made to determine if an intervention is appropriate for a particular family.

The assessment

The assessment begins during the first conversation between the interventionist and one or more of the family members or concerned persons. In making an assessment, the interventionist should consider thoroughly the following questions:

- Does the information (data) from the concerned persons indicate that the person being discussed is dependent?

- What are the motives of the interveners? Do they appear to be acting out of love and concern, or are there ulterior motives which could make the intervention a risky, possibly dangerous route to take?

- Do the concerned persons have enough strength of purpose and emotional stability to follow through on the suggested process of guided intervention?

- Are some or all of the concerned persons willing to be involved in treatment after the intervention?

- Is the family willing to follow through on homework assignments such as reading and attending AA and Al-Anon meetings?

- Will family members carefully consider — and visit if possible — treatment programs which might be appropriate for the dependent?

- Is it the family's goal to use the intervention merely as a means to get the dependent to stop using, or do the co-dependents recognize the need for treatment and aftercare? Remember, interventions are *not* designed just to stop people from using chemicals. The goal of interventions is to motivate dependents and families to begin the recovery process through treatment.

If the interventionist concludes that a guided intervention may be helpful, but the family does not complete the pre-intervention assignments, the specialist should reassess whether the technique is appropriate. If the family members' dedication to change is weak, they may need help to develop the requisite strength to participate constructively in an intervention.

In addition to answering the concerns listed here, interventionists should consider the possibility of physical or sexual abuse in the family. Increasing evidence in the last decade shows a disproportionate incidence of violence, including incest, in chemically dependent families. Also, chemical dependency is very likely to develop in one or more members of a family in which battering or sexual abuse takes place. The abuse will not necessarily cease when the abuser stops drinking or taking drugs. Even upon successful completion of treatment, chemically dependent victims of abuse may go back to their old habits if they continue to be victimized by other family members after their return home. Specialists in chemical dependency and sexual abuse recognize that the problems are usually so entwined that it is necessary to treat both areas for the family to recover from either.

During the assessment, a member of the family may describe physical or sexual abuse taking place within the family. If after sensitive and direct questioning the interventionist confirms that abuses are occuring, he or she must:

- Explain to the family that human service professionals are required by law to report the situation to the state or county social services department or child abuse agency — and do so. In this difficult task, interventionists can provide an important service.

- Offer support to the victim(s) of abuse and encourage the individual or family to plan an effective confrontation with the perpetrator, with the aid of a trained person from the appropriate agency.

- Determine the appropriate time for a chemical dependency intervention. Should this be postponed until the physical or sexual abuse has stopped? Or is there little hope of stopping the abuse while the abuser is still using alcohol or drugs? Are family members in immediate danger? The key considera- tion is family safety. The interventionist should determine whether a referral to a local battered women's shelter or similar "safe house" is appropriate.

Frequently the interventionist may suspect that physical and/or sexual abuse is occuring, even though family members deny these problems. In these cases, too, the interventionist is legally bound to report this belief to the agency dealing with abuse and neglect. He or she should also report these suspicions to the family, and, if the dependent goes into treatment, to the treatment center staff. Every professional has a respon- sibility to report well-founded suspicions of neglect or physical or sexual abuse.

Assault interventions are different from chemical dependency interventions. For example, rarely would a family — not to mention friends or employers — be assembled to confront a man about an incestuous relationship with his daughter. Social service profes- sionals usually are best qualified to guide this kind of intervention.

Preparing for the intervention

Educating the family

First, the family must be educated so that co-depend- ents go into the intervention — and ultimately into treatment — with an understanding of the dynamics of the dependency they are battling. They probably will need to shed their old assumptions about chemical dependency and learn concepts which will be important to the success of the intervention and subsequent treatment. The following points should be reviewed carefully with the family:

- Chemical dependency is a treatable disease with certain predictable symptoms. It is not a moral problem or the result of a weak will.

- Dependents, except in rare cases, are incapable of initiating their own recovery. The sicker they get, the less likely it is they will be able to do so.

- The disease is not just the dependent's problem. A co-dependent's life is as unmanageable as the dependent's. Co-dependents are truly powerless over the dependent's behavior and use of chemicals. This concept — along with an understanding of chemical dependency as a treatable disease — is central to the preparation of a successful intervention. A discussion of family roles, enabling behaviors, and the purposes of Al-Anon and Alateen can lead family members to better understand co-dependency.

- Co-dependents must make a commitment to change the ways in which they enable the dependents to continue using their chemicals. They must be willing to participate in a recovery program.

- Recovery is a lifelong process. Guided intervention initiates the process but, by itself, it is not enough.

Preparation of the family for this carefully controlled crisis should include some homework assignments. Co-dependents should be encouraged to make a list of their own enabling behaviors and share them with the others. They should attend open AA and Al-Anon meetings to help them understand that other families react to their dependents in similar ways and that their feelings are not unique. The meetings also will help to prepare them for family treatment.

Whether or not the intervention succeeds in getting the dependent into treatment, it can be the beginning of recovery for other family members. The process offers them an opportunity to understand and to cease enabling behaviors, and to start building healthier relationships with one another.

Choosing the intervention team

Another important part of the planning process is selecting the intervention team.

Ideally, the team is comprised of people representing different areas of the dependent's life — home, busi-ness, social, medical, spiritual, and others. A dependent has more trouble rationalizing or minimizing input when it comes from a variety of sources.

Intervention teams vary from one or two members to a dozen or more, with an average of six to ten. There are dangers in forming a team with more than a dozen people. The intervention process demands careful con-trol, which may be impossible to maintain with a large group. The power of intimacy can be lost when there are too many people in the room. On the other hand, if the group is very small, there is a risk that its impact will not be enough to convince the dependent to accept treatment.

Parents frequently want to exclude children from an intervention. But children suffer from being part of a chemically dependent family, so it is appropriate that they share in the beginning of family healing. The intervention is likely to be the family's first honest communication for a long time.

Some children resist participation. Unless they change their minds during the preparation phase, they should not be forced to attend the actual intervention. A child may choose to participate by writing a letter to be read aloud at the intervention. Certainly, children can be very effective in motivating the dependent to accept treatment.

Interventions can succeed with just one or two team members, but interventionists should make certain that others are not being excluded out of fear or shame. For example, Cynthia attempted to hide her husband's alcoholism for years. When she decided that an intervention was necessary and could be effective, she tried to keep it a secret by limiting the team to two close friends. She later admitted she was afraid of others' scorn and gossip.

Oscar, whose wife, Bethany, was a polydrug abuser (she abused more than one mood-altering drug), fought to involve only the immediate family — even though he'd talked about the problem to family friends and his minister. "I thought our family should handle it alone. I was ashamed to ask for help from others, even though I knew they cared. Thank God, the counselor prevailed. The intervention was a success, partly because Bethany knew I'd already discussed the problem with our friends. And the others were wonderful support for my daughters and me."

The following criteria may be used to determine whether an individual, adult or child, should be on the intervention team:

- Does the individual care about the dependent?

- Is this person significant in the dependent's life? The significance may be emotional, financial, spiritual, or psychological.

- Is the individual likely to follow the prescribed format of the intervention, or is there a danger that he or she will jeopardize the process with angry outbursts, inappropriate questions, or deviations from the established procedure?

- Does this person have specific information which will be useful in the intervention? Occasionally an individual may be included who does not have specific knowledge about the dependent's use but can serve an important function on the team. For example, an employer may not have any first-hand knowledge of the situation but can offer reassurance that the dependent's job will be protected if treatment is accepted.

Other special members of the team may be the "surprise guest" and the "kicker," terms coined by Linda Scott, author of the *Intervention Guide*.

The surprise guest is a member of the intervention team whose presence can have a positive impact on the dependent, perhaps a favorite out-of-town aunt, an old friend from high school, a college roommate, or two boys from the Cub Scout troop. The surprise guest generally serves to keep the dependent on his best behavior and promotes a special feeling of concern and affection.

The kicker is someone who is unable to be present in person at the intervention but who is willing to contribute a recorded tape, letter, or phone call. Such contributions can be powerful additions to an intervention. They show that concern for the dependent is widespread and that the "secret" is not a secret at all.

What if a team member also has a problem with alcohol or other drugs? An interventionist may suspect that a member of the intervention team may also be a chemical dependent. Prospective team members may be asked to complete the questionnaire on page 111 and their responses should be assessed carefully. Although anyone who might jeopardize the chances for success should be excluded, some people with chemical problems can play a productive part in an intervention.

During one intervention, the dependent challenged his brother Tom's drinking. Tom took a deep breath and replied, "Bud, in the last couple of weeks I've done some thinking. To tell you the truth, I'm a little scared for myself. Maybe I need one of these meetings too. But this morning we're here for you. We love you and want you to get help, so please hear us out, okay?" The intervention proceeded, and Bud entered treatment that morning. Subsequently an intervention was arranged for his brother, who was relieved to be confronted at last with his own problem.

Choosing a time

There are a few factors to consider in scheduling the actual time of the intervention:

- It is extremely important that the dependent be sober and straight during the intervention. Since some dependents use chemicals almost continuously, this may present logistical problems. The morning after a particularly bad night is an ideal time, and co-dependents often can anticipate this situation.

- Many treatment programs require admission during a specified time of the week or day. This should be researched after the team has decided on a treatment program. It would be unwise, for example, to schedule an intervention for a Friday afternoon if the treatment center could not admit the dependent until the following Monday. The less time that elapses between the intervention and treatment, the better. Ideally, the dependent can be taken directly from the intervention to treatment.

- Team members should allow sufficient time for the intervention and a follow-up debriefing. The total time required is usually less than three hours.

Choosing a setting

The intervention should be held in a place where the dependent will be able to listen, undisturbed, and really hear the others' love and concern. Generally, the dependent's home should *not* be used. Phone calls, unexpected visitors, distracting pets, and trips to the bathroom, liquor cabinet, or medicine chest obviously can threaten the success of an intervention. Besides, a dependent is more likely to manipulate the participants and sabotage an intervention if it takes place at home. He or she may even order the team to leave! Of course, if a dependent never leaves home or is temporarily bedridden, it may be necessary to carry the intervention to the dependent. Usually, the office of the interventionist or the dependent's minister, doctor, employer, or another team member is preferable to a home setting. Experienced interventionists sometimes do successful interventions in people's homes, especially when employers are willing to participate.

Wherever the intervention takes place, the setting must be comfortable and private so the intervention can proceed without outside disturbance. No unplanned phone calls or visitors should be permitted.

Getting the dependent there

Family members worry about whether they can get the dependent to the intervention. But most counselors agree that the question should be not *whether* but *how* to get the dependent there. Once an intervention team is committed and prepared, a solution can be found. A few examples:

- Joyce's employer requested a Monday morning meeting with her. When she entered the office, she found her family, several friends, and the interventionist waiting for her.

- Arthur's family told him in advance that they were seeking help for their problems coping with his drinking. After they completed all necessary planning and preparation sessions with the interventionist, they asked Arthur to join them for one session.

- Kathy's mother called her on the telephone and asked her to come to her apartment. When Kathy asked, "Why? What's the matter?" her mother responded vaguely, but truthfully, "There's a real crisis we have to talk about, but I'd rather talk about it when you get here. Please come over right away."

Many dependents who enter treatment as a result of an intervention report that the confrontation was not entirely a surprise. One reason is that, in the process of preparing for the intervention, team members often stop some of their enabling behaviors. They give up trying to control the dependent's drug or alcohol use, and they stop shielding the dependent from consequences. Some dependents recognize these clues and suspect something is going on.

Choosing a treatment program

As mentioned previously, the interventionist may find it necessary to dispel the team's unrealistic hope that the intervention alone will serve as treatment. Families and dependents often try to go it alone using the "white knuckle" approach; the dependent abstains from the alcohol and other drug use but neither the dependent nor any other family member changes the related behaviors. This is not treatment and the chance for recovery is slim.

The selection of a treatment program requires research and careful consideration. The choice should be made by the intervention team with the guidance of the professional counselor. First, the interventionist should talk with family members about their expectations and explain the treatment options to them. In order to make realistic recommendations for treatment the interventionist should ask the family to check insurance coverage.

It has been demonstrated that one-to-one counseling alone is seldom effective treatment for chemical dependency. Group support and confrontation offer dependents a better chance for recovery. The interventionist should explain that chemical dependency treatment is specialized counseling. The goals are:

- First, to help dependents confront the fact that their lives have become unmanageable because of alcohol or drug use, and that they are truly powerless to control the chemical. This is also the First Step of the Twelve Step Program of Alcoholics Anonymous (AA).

- Second, treatment strives to motivate dependents to get well.

- Third, it teaches "tools of recovery" which are necessary for sustained abstinence. The most successful programs combine education, group therapy, individual counseling, and the introduction of the dependent and the family to the fellowships of

AA, Al-Anon, or other appropriate self-help groups.

- Finally, treatment should provide a structure for establishing healthy lifestyle patterns. Exercise and nutrition programs can be designed for each dependent. Yoga, meditation, stress management, and expressive therapies such as role-playing can add depth to a program's services. However, it is important to remember that good treatment focuses first on developing the dependent's capacity to stay straight and sober.

Inpatient treatment provides a safe environment and an intensive program for the patient to begin recovery. It frees the dependent from daily responsibilities and the pressure of relationships, and it allows the dependent to participate fully in intensive group therapy sessions, discussions, and activities. Inpatient treatment is almost always recommended if the dependent has a long history of use or has failed in several attempts to stop abusing chemicals. Dependents with medical complications, including the possibility of health-threatening withdrawal, should be referred to inpatient treatment. Inpatient treatment also is indicated if the family is unable or unwilling to offer support.

Outpatient treatment is generally less expensive and is often effective with early-stage dependents who can maintain their normal responsibilities and be counted on to abstain from all mood-altering chemicals during treatment.

Some dependents begin their recovery not in formal

treatment programs but in AA or NA. These fellow-ships provide excellent long-term support for dependents; however, their effectiveness often is enhanced if dependents first complete a treatment program.

If at all possible, family members should visit local treatment resources before reaching a decision about the best program for the dependent and themselves.

The rehearsal and final plans

Purpose of the rehearsal

The pre-intervention rehearsal may be the first time all concerned people meet as an intervention team. All individuals who will be participating at the intervention must be at this meeting.

The rehearsal serves several major functions:

- It helps the team anticipate what the intervention may actually be like. Team members present their data to an empty chair. Some interventionists prefer to have a a volunteer who is a recovering dependent role-play the dependent.

- It gives participants a sense of what feelings may emerge during the intervention. Some participants understandably feel a great deal of anger. These feelings will be explored during treatment, but team members should be able to put them aside during an intervention. A show of anger can be destructive because it triggers the dependent's defenses.

- It allows team members to focus on feelings of

love and concern for the dependent, for each other, and for themselves. These positive feelings provide indispensable momentum to the intervention process.

- It offers participants an opportunity to deal with their fears, concerns, and questions about the intervention itself.

- It helps participants gain confidence and define their roles in the intervention.

- It provides the team with a chance to discuss contingencies or anticipate trouble that may arise during the actual intervention. If the interventionist believes the team needs more time to prepare, the intervention should be postponed.

Data-sharing

The success of the intervention will be influenced largely by the way concerns and data are presented. Therefore, it is crucial for interventionists to review the data and instruct participants in how to share information about the dependent's problem in a way that will be fully heard.

Data should demonstrate the powerlessness of the dependent over mood-altering substances. It also should show, through specific examples, the unmanageability of the dependent's life due to chemical use, and the effects of the dependency on other people.

Other guidelines for presenting information to the dependent:

- Data should be written so that participants can refer to their lists. This can help team members to "stick to the facts" in the emotionally charged atmosphere of the intervention.

- Three complete copies of each person's written data should be prepared and brought to the intervention. One copy should be given to the dependent, whether or not treatment is accepted. Another should be given to the dependent's treatment counselor, and the team member should keep the third copy.

- Data should be non-judgmental and specific. The team member should include the date and time of an incident, who was there, what happened, and his or her own feelings about it.

- The words "alcoholic" and "addict" and similar diagnostic terms should be omitted from the intervention. They provoke a "porcupine response" and rarely serve a useful purpose. Participants and the interventionist should speak in plain language, and avoid psychological jargon.

- Whenever possible, recent incidents should be reported. Fresh data usually has more emotional impact and is less likely to bring forth justifications from the dependent. Of course, old problems associated with use may be raised, but the dependent may minimize or rationalize those incidents. ("Well, I've certainly changed since *those* days!")

71

- Five or six incidents are generally the maximum required from each team member.

- Team members should affirm their conviction that the dependent needs professional help in order to overcome the problems associated with chemical use. This should be done lovingly and assertively.

- Intervention participants should make eye contact with and speak directly to the dependent.

Here are some examples of data:

- "Sylvia, last Saturday you told me you were never going to have a drink again, but when I saw you at the office party you had a drink in your hand and were talking loudly about how a drink now and then never hurt anybody."

- "Rolf, last Monday afternoon I sent you home because you were high on pot. You handle danger-ous machinery at the plant and have been cited twice for safety infractions."

Before the last pre-intervention meeting ends, the team should confirm seating arrangements. Thoughtful planning will assure that the dependent sits close to those who have a calming influence, perhaps on a comfortable couch away from the door. The speaking order for the intervention also should be planned: start with someone who is respected by the dependent and who is strong enough to withstand any initial resist-ance. It is generally effective to end the data-sharing phase of the intervention with a fervent plea — usually from a close family member — that the dependent seek help.

The "what if" clause and ultimatums

Participants, with the help of the interventionist, will need to discuss and to agree on a team response if the dependent refuses treatment. For example, the dependent may reject the recommendation for treatment but promise to abstain from futher use of all mood-altering chemicals.

Through the "what if" clause the team asks the dependent to agree to the recommended treatment if and when he or she resumes chemical use. Or, if the dependent refuses the specified treatment, the intervention team may present a different treatment option to the dependent. Alternative treatment should be offered only if it appears to be genuinely appropriate.

Some interventionists prefer that team members share ultimatums with dependents whether or not they agree to treatment; others prefer to withhold ultimatums unless they're needed as leverage to convince dependents to accept treatment. Though our preference is usually the latter, we urge the team to share ultimatums with the dependent during treatment, at a time when they can be discussed in depth. Ultimatums have two main purposes:

- They may create the kind of crisis that will cause the dependent to agree to go into treatment. (Remember, dependents very seldom seek help for themselves until a crisis forces them to do so.)

- They help team members confront their own enabling behaviors as well as ways in which they
  suffer with the dependent.

All ultimatums must be carefully considered and
discussed in advance of the intervention. Participants
must be prepared to follow through on ultimatums if
necessary. The dependent probably has heard dozens
of threats in the past, and like a child who learns to
laugh off the idle warnings of parents, knows they
seldom materialize. The formality of the intervention
may influence the dependent to believe ultimatums,
but it's just as important that team members also take
them seriously.

Because situations and people are so different, strin-
gent guidelines for ultimatums are impossible. The
following examples of ultimatums were appropriate for
one intervention team:

- "Harold, you are one of my best friends. I care
  about you a lot, but I can no longer sit by and
  watch you destroy yourself. It's not fun playing
  tennis with you anymore. Unless you accept your
  need for help, I'm going to find a new partner."

- "Dad, we love you. Unless you enter the treatment
  program we are recommending, our family will no
  longer join you and Mom for the Christmas holidays. It's too painful for us to watch your
  disintegration."

- "Harold, you are a valued employee, and I want to keep you in the firm. However, if you do not accept our recommendation for treatment, you are not welcome back on the job."

In these examples team members are telling Harold clearly what action they will take if he refuses treatment. Ultimatums should be concise, honest statements rather than emotional threats.

The intervention

An intervention is the culmination of much soul-searching, discussion, and planning. As on the opening night of a theatrical production, the cast is likely to be nervous. But the stage has been set, the music written, and the production rehearsed. If the team members follow their scripts carefully, there will be a minimum of confusion and a maximum of positive impact.

An interventionist who has adequately prepared the team should play a small role in the actual intervention. When all participants and the dependent are assembled, the dependent should first be apprised of the interventionist's identity, specialty, and function in the group. The interventionist can accomplish this with a simple explanation. In addition, the interventionist should ask the dependent to agree to the procedures previously established by the team. The interventionist should communicate through words, tone, and attitude the care and concern which is so vital to the success of the intervention.

The intervention should follow, as closely as possible, the plans which were carefully discussed and rehearsed.

It is best to begin the data-sharing as soon as possible and to keep the process moving along according to the plan. If necessary, the dependent may be reminded of the agreement to hear each person out. Although spontaneity during the intervention may have a powerful impact, it is highly unpredictable and usually should be controlled. A guided intervention is not group therapy, nor is it an appropriate context for a freewheeling exploration of feelings, nor an examination of interpersonal dynamics. If team members digress into these kinds of explorations, the interventionist should gently but firmly intercede and bring the focus back to data-sharing and simple expressions of love, concern, and hope.

If the dependent refuses to accept the recommendation for treatment, the interventionist should not assume that this is a final decision. The defenses of chemically dependent people are often so tough that it is necessary for the intervention team to chisel away through persistent reminders of failed attempts to control use of chemicals. When it appears that ultimatums or the "what if" clause may serve a useful purpose, the interventionist should invite the team to use them.

Often a dependent will question the interventionist, sometimes out of a genuine desire for information or a tacit respect for the interventionist's specialty. Such questions should be answered directly, although the interventionist also may want to turn to team members for amplification. For example, if the dependent asks, "What will happen at this treatment center, anyway?" the interventionist may describe succinctly the recommended treatment program, but also may ask one or two of the team members to describe their visit to the center and their impressions of the program.

Sometimes a dependent will fire questions at the interventionist in an attempt to derail the confrontation. In this situation, the interventionist should ask the dependent to hold questions until others have finished and to adhere to the previously agreed upon procedure established by the team.

If the dependent leaves the room, one or two team members should go along. Although dependents rarely refuse to return to the room, the intervention team should decide ahead of time what to do if this happens. In some cases, the intervention can be moved to another place. In others it may be necessary for members to follow the dependent and present their ultimatums. This helps build a crisis which may make the dependent more likely to accept the need for treatment.

If the dependent leaves the intervention prematurely, or stays but refuses to enter treatment, the interventionist should encourage the team to avoid enabling behaviors. Team members will find that the rehearsal and the intervention have been useful in helping them examine their own roles and feelings about the dependent's use. Ideally, they will use this knowledge to help themselves, and possibly, the dependent.

With adequate preparation and with a prevailing attitude of love, concern, and hope, the intervention team will almost surely lead the dependent to accept the team's recommendation. Experienced interventionists report an 80 to 90 percent success rate using this approach.

The follow-up

We have said that an intervention is a many-phased process beginning with the assessment. The final phase of this process, the follow-up, is extremely important. Up to this point, team members have been compelled to take a close look at their relationship to the dependent and to each other. They have learned about a serious disease and how it affects them. Finally, the intervention has penetrated the wall built by the "no talk" rule, but without continued vigilance the rule quickly will be reestablished. If this happens, the family will come to view the intervention as an aberration, and the commitments made during the process will be twisted in memory rather than honored. Team members must be willing, collectively and individually, to continue their efforts for honest, open communication with the dependent and among themselves.

One way to encourage this openness is for the interventionist to arrange a follow-up session with the team. Even in the afterglow of a successful intervention, team members may feel a residual guilt at "betraying" the dependent or "putting him (or her) through it." At the follow-up meeting, they can discuss the intervention and their feelings about it. The interventionist should be aware that a family system changes considerably when the dependent is sober and straight. Although family members desperately want the dependent to stop using chemicals, they may be frightened or unaware of how much the newfound sobriety will alter their lives. They may feel overwhelmed and confused. In the Herrara family, for example, Albert's twin daughters were born after he became hooked on cocaine. In the five years which passed before he entered treatment, they had established enabling behaviors and learned how to accommodate their father's erratic conduct. They became accustomed to their parents' arguments and ways of dealing with each other. When Albert came home after successful completion of his treatment program, he seemed almost like a stranger to the little girls. They found his new behavior disconcerting. They didn't know how to talk to him or what to expect from him. Family treatment would have been very useful to them — even at their young age.

The interventionist can be of great service to the dependent by staying in contact during the treatment phase. It is wise to ask the family to sign release-of-information forms so that data presented during the intervention can be discussed with treatment program counselors working with the dependent. This data can help break through the dependent's denial, which may become re-established as treatment begins.

Some specialists provide ongoing support groups for families who have participated in interventions. Ideally, families are integrated into the dependent's treatment program and aftercare plan. Al-Anon and Alateen also offer invaluable support.

Part three
Intervention: The application

6
Intervention experiences

The following, from the experiences of professional interventionists and told from the interventionist's point of view, are based on interventions which actually happened and which helped to turn people's lives around. Although the families and individuals involved gave their permission for us to recount these experiences — in the hope that others might be helped through the same technique of intervention — details have been changed to protect their anonymity.

Clark, a 43-year-old alcoholic

Mary called me early one Monday morning distraught after her husband's wild drinking binge over the weekend. She wasn't convinced that Clark was an alcoholic, but she was sure that drinking influenced his behavior. She described how she and their children were sick of Clark's broken promises, frightened by his drunk driving, and worried that he might explode in anger and hurt someone. She asked how she could tell if he was an alcoholic, and she sought my advice on whether she should threaten to leave home with the children if he did not stop drinking.

I asked Mary if she had made similar threats in the past. She replied dismally that she had, but without much success. Clark's drinking, it seemed to her, had worsened during the past couple of years. She described several incidents which made it clear that her husband Clark was indeed dependent on alcohol.

I suggested that we get together to explore her options. Before our meeting, I asked her to write a list of specific instances in which Clark's drinking resulted in a problem for himself or someone else, and to include dates, times, places, what happened, and how she felt about the incidents.

I also requested that she ask other people who were concerned about Clark's drinking to come to our meeting. She balked about bringing other people into a discussion of Clark's drinking. She named several relatives and friends who cared about Clark and who knew about his alcohol problem, but she was hesitant about asking any of them except her daughter Robin to come. We agreed to get together the next afternoon.

When Mary and Robin arrived at my office, we talked about Clark's drinking and how it had affected him and his family. They told me that Clark had been arrested twice for driving while intoxicated, had a history of leaving jobs suddenly, and often became violently angry while drunk. Mary said their family physician had warned Clark that his liver functions were abnormal. She described how Clark had withdrawn from church and social activities which the family had enjoyed together in previous years. He had made several attempts to stop drinking, and once spent two days in a detoxification center.

In spite of all this, Mary and Robin were not convinced that Clark was an alcoholic. Robin seemed to feel that they were responsible for his drinking, and they wondered whether there might be something they could do to make life easier so Clark would stay sober. They felt helpless, as though their own lives were out of control. At times they even felt *they* were going crazy.

I gave Mary and Robin some basic information about alcoholism and invited them to view two films with other families the following evening. I also described the process of guided intervention to them. They said they would consider using the technique to confront Clark about the reality of his (and their) situation and to get some effective help for the whole family. We discussed the guilt they felt in talking with me "behind his back," but at the same time they both knew that Clark was not receptive to open discussion about his drinking and that it was impossible for them to deal with the problem by themselves. Mary still did not want to involve her ten-year-old son, Tim. I suggested that she postpone this decision for a day or two.

The following evening, while Tim was at a friend's house and Clark was out with his buddies, Mary and Robin returned to my office. They saw the films, *The Family Trap* and *I'll Quit Tomorrow*. They also talked with some other people who were considering interventions for family members.

I described in greater detail the rationale for and the process of guided intervention. We talked about their feelings of guilt and shame, their powerlessness, the unmanageability of their lives, and their fears.

By the end of the evening Mary and Robin had decided an intervention was appropriate. Mary agreed to include Tim on the intervention team, and she listed other people who were worried about Clark and cared enough about him and the family to join in. Clark's brother, who lived in the same town, and his sister, who lived several hundred miles away, would be invited to participate. Mary also thought Clark's best friend might be willing to help. He was a "hard drinker" himself but had said more than once that sometimes Clark got out of control and should "slow down." Mary thought their family doctor would be too busy to attend the required planning meeting and the intervention, but agreed to ask him anyway. The manager of the local bowling alley was another possibility. He and Clark had been friends for a long time, and he had witnessed some horrendous scenes caused by Clark's drinking. In fact, twice he had called the police.

Mary felt sure Clark's employer would fire him if his "secret" became known, but when she made an anonymous call to inquire about the company's policy on retaining alcoholics after treatment, she discovered that Clark's employer had an excellent employee assistance program. When Mary summoned up her courage to tell Clark's supervisor about Clark's drinking, she was surprised to learn that he was already aware of the problem. He agreed to join the intervention team.

The team eventually consisted of Mary, Robin, Tim, Clark's brother, sister, brother-in-law, the bowling alley manager, the family minister, and Clark's supervisor. The family physician was unable to attend, but he wrote a letter to be read by the minister during the intervention. Clark's drinking pal refused to take part, but he agreed not to tell Clark about the plans.

Clark's brother and Mary visited two treatment centers and attended an open meeting of AA. Mary and her children also attended Al-Anon and Alateen meetings, and the entire intervention team was given reading material to help them prepare for the intervention. Clark's supervisor checked the insurance coverage and made arrangements to handle Clark's absence from the office.

One week after Mary's phone call, on the afternoon before the scheduled intervention, the entire team met with me. All agreed that the intervention should have a tone of "tough love." They were determined to avoid angry confrontations and to follow the plan of forcefully recommending treatment at a local inpatient program. If Clark refused to enter treatment, his supervisor would tell him that the firm felt strongly enough about his need for help to terminate his employment unless he agreed. Clark's sister and brother-in-law would tell him he would not be welcome at the upcoming Labor Day Weekend family reunion if he refused treatment. Mary planned to tell him that she was unwilling to subject herself and the children to his abuse when he was drunk, and that if he refused treatment they would immediately move out of the house to stay with his brother. The children agreed to support this ultimatum.

During the preliminary meeting, the team rehearsed the intervention. An associate of mine played the role of Clark and, one by one, team members read their lists to him. Each person concluded with a personal statement to the effect that "I care about you and want you to get help."

The bowling alley manager became angry and judgmental during the rehearsal. We discussed how this could jeopardize the intervention, and I stressed the need for Clark to feel the group's love and concern. The manager said he would try to put aside his anger during the intervention, and I felt he could do it.

Also during this meeting Mary and her children became more decisive about their own need for help. Mary and her brother-in-law had chosen a treatment program which offered an excellent family component, and she believed Al-Anon would provide her with invaluable support. She and the children now seemed genuinely committed to doing something about their own problems. But would they be able to convince Clark to get help?

The following morning Mary told Clark that she and the children had been seeing a counselor and needed him to attend the next session. Clark became angry and accused her of trying to turn the children against him, but he said he would go along to "set the record straight." It already had been decided that if he refused to attend, his supervisor would call and ask him to come to work for an emergency meeting. As it happened, he and the family arrived in my office on time. The rest of the intervention team had assembled, each person sitting in a previously agreed upon chair. They were nervous, but fully prepared to carry out the intervention.

When Clark entered the room, the color drained from his face, but he did not explode in anger as his family had feared. Instead, he sighed deeply and sat down quietly. He appeared not to recognize the team members as individuals.

I introduced myself and said, "I have been asked by your family and the others here today to help them tell you how concerned they are about your drinking. They want to tell you about the problems it is causing you — and them. I'd like you to listen to what they have to say. After they've spoken, we will give you an opportunity to respond. Are you willing to listen to them?"

We knew that Clark might leave. Had this happened, Clark's brother and supervisor would have followed him out and asked him to return. Instead, Clark seemed temporarily overwhelmed and simply nodded his head in assent. He glanced nervously around the room, focusing for just an instant on each person. The emotional impact on him was so strong that he did not even greet his sister and brother-in-law whom he had not seen for months. Nor did he speak to anyone else. He looked away from Timmy, who was crying quietly.

I asked Clark's brother to begin. He unfolded a piece of paper and began to read. "Clark, last Tuesday when we went out to dinner, you had three doubles and two beers. You spilled your water over my dinner and began talking so loudly that the maitre d' came over to ask you to be quieter. I was angry and embarrassed for you — and for me." He related three other incidents, stressing facts rather than his own judgments. He closed by saying, "I care for you and I'm worried about you.

You've told me several times that you were going to stop drinking, but you haven't been able to do it for very long. I want you to agree to get help."

Clark spoke for the first time since entering my office. "Okay, I hear you. I know what the rest of you are going to say. I have been hitting it a little hard. That's why I came in here this morning. I want us to get counseling. I'm willing, okay?"

At this point, Mary could have accurately pointed out that Clark was angry earlier when she asked him to come to the session. She and the other team members could have responded that he had been hitting it more than "a little hard." These responses might have led to arguments which would have derail the intervention. I merely said, "Clark, I'd like you to listen to what the others have to say. Reverend?"

The minister read the letter from Clark's physician and then spoke from his notes, listing incidents in which Clark's drinking had caused problems. He closed his presentation by saying that he hoped Clark would accept help.

One by one the team members expressed deep concern about Clark based on their first-hand knowledge of problems associated with his alcohol use. Robin brought tears to everyone's eyes when she recounted the anguish she felt when Clark, while drunk, made fun of her in front of her friends. She described the anger and confusion she felt the next day when he denied the incident had even happened.

Clark broke down as Robin finished with her plea that he accept help. "What do you want me to do?"

Mary answered, "Clark, we want you to enter the alcoholism recovery center at the hospital. Timmy and Robin and I will take part too, in the family program. Your brother and I went there and met the counselors.

We like the place and it has a good reputation. Our insurance will pay for it," she added.

"How long would I have to be there?" He looked at me.

I answered him. "The average length of stay is about a month. Your family will participate with you for a full week."

"A month? No way! I can't take off from work that long."

Clark's supervisor promised Clark that his job would be held for him if he completed the treatment program, and said arrangements had been made to handle Clark's work load in his absence.

Timmy added: "Do it, Daddy. Do it. We want you to get well."

Clark, now overcome with emotion, said "okay," repeating the word over and over again. Mary and Clark's sister hugged him, and others reached out to each other, wrung out, tearful, but happy with the outcome.

Clark entered the treatment program that night. He has been sober since 1981 and his family is doing well.

Each intervention is unique, of course. Some are considerably stormier and more argumentative than Clark's. However, if the team is well prepared, most contingencies can be anticipated, allowing the intervention to proceed to a successful conclusion.

Jaimie, a 16-year-old polydrug dependent

Susan called me on the advice of a school counselor who suggested that her son, Jaimie, should be evaluated for a possible drug problem.

Jaimie was a troubled 16-year-old. When his mother came to my office, she described Jaimie's fights in school and around the neighborhood. She said he rarely attended classes, often stayed out past his curfew, and was verbally abusive.

Jaimie had been "busted" by school officials for pot smoking, and he had been suspended twice for drinking at school. After the suspensions, Susan searched his room and found beer cans, marijuana seeds, and several pills she couldn't identify. She didn't say anything to Jaimie because she was afraid of his reaction.

Susan didn't know whether Jaimie's problems were related to his chemical use. She knew he had tried marijuana, but naively doubted he used other drugs. She was unable to explain the pills she'd seen in Jaimie's desk. This denial of the scope of the problem is all too common among parents of adolescents.

In our first interview, Susan could not describe any instances in which her son's chemical use had caused a problem for himself or others. However, it seemed likely that Jaimie was harmfully involved with chemicals, and that a full assessment was appropriate. Susan listed several people who knew Jaimie well, including his school counselor, a psychologist he'd seen briefly, his boss at the supermarket, a former friend who had gone through a drug treatment program, and his girlfriend.

I described the chemical dependency assessment procedure (see page 55) and asked Susan to invite the people she had mentioned to a meeting. I also asked Susan to have Jaimie's school counselor contact me, hoping he would be able to shed more light on Jaimie's involvement with drugs and alcohol. Although limited by the necessity for confidentiality, the counselor described several incidents in which Jaimie's involvement with drugs was evident.

The assessment meeting took place several days later, and it was clear Jaimie had problems with chemicals. His girlfriend, Kelly, wept as she related incident after incident in which Jaimie's involvement with drugs had frightened her. Susan listened incredulously as Kelly recounted how Jaimie had broken into several homes to steal jewelry and stereo equipment which he pawned to pay for his drug habit. Kelly also described his dangerous driving and erratic behavior.

His boss said Jaimie had quit his job earlier in the week after he was caught smoking pot in the meat freezer. Others told of their concerns. Peter, the youth who had been in a chemical dependency treatment program, said Jaimie had asked him how to get off drugs. But Peter also related that Jaimie had quickly minimized and rationalized his chemical use, saying, "I can stop any time I want."

After the assessment, Susan attended an Al-Anon meeting and visited several treatment programs. Initially, she had hoped that one-to-one counseling and more discipline at home would put an end to Jaimie's drug use, but she gradually came to understand that Jaimie needed to be immersed in a program with other adolescents struggling with many of the same issues.

Some intervention team members were pessimistic; they doubted that Jaimie would agree to treatment or even remain in the room during the intervention. For this reason, they had to consider what they would do if Jaimie left the intervention or refused treatment. They decided that if he left, Peter and Kelly would follow him and try to get him to return. The group planned to wait a half-hour before calling off the intervention.

Susan believed it was important for Jaimie to enter treatment voluntarily, because if forced, he would surely run away. If Jaimie refused voluntary treatment, the group decided to give him the option of abstaining from all mood-altering chemicals with the stipulation that he would submit to periodic blood tests. If the tests showed he was using again, either he would enter the recommended treatment center or be committed to the locked ward of another chemical dependency treatment program.

After three planning sessions, including a rehearsal, the intervention team was ready to confront Jaimie. The morning of the intervention, Susan told Jaimie she had scheduled a meeting with a counselor. Jaimie was surly when he arrived at my office with his mother, and the session was stormy. He ran out as soon as I told him why we were gathered. Peter and Kelly, as planned, followed him and persuaded him to return to the room. He grudgingly re-entered the meeting, warning, "You're not going to make me do anything. I can take off anytime I want."

Despite his belligerence, Jaimie sat down and we started with the data-sharing phase of the intervention. He interrupted frequently and tried to sabotage the intervention with abusive remarks. He vehemently refused to enter treatment, so Susan told him if he didn't stop drinking and using drugs and if he refused to submit to blood tests, she would send him to a locked facility. Jaimie sneered, and replied, "All right, all right. I'll stop. It's not that big a deal." On that note, the session ended.

Two days later, Susan told Jaimie she was taking him to have a blood test. He responded, "Save your money. I know what it will show — I was out partying last night." Fortunately, Susan was well prepared to carry out her ultimatum. She told Jaimie he had to enter a treatment program immediately. He refused. As she started to call the sheriff's department to get help in transporting Jaimie to a locked facility, Jaimie broke down and sobbed. He was almost incoherent when he screamed at Susan, "Okay. Just get off my back and I'll go to the damn treatment center."

Jaimie was admitted to the voluntary program that afternoon. During his first week in treatment, he complained often and threatened to leave. But day by day, he became more motivated to turn his life around. He felt the support of other adolescents going through similar experiences, and he responded well to the professional counseling program.

After three months, Jaimie was ready to go home. He relapsed several times after leaving treatment, but he has been straight for four years. Today, Jaimie is a counselor at a runaway house for adolescents.

Jaimie's intervention was successful because people who cared about him were willing to risk his anger and because his mother used her leverage to insist that he enter treatment.

Eleanor, a 74-year-old alcoholic and prescription drug dependent

Eleanor was admitted to the hospital for extensive tests. She was at the point of exhaustion — frail, malnourished, and weak. She denied drinking more than a "sip or two at a party now and then." However, she was obviously intoxicated when she entered the hospital, and the admitting physician ordered a blood alcohol test which showed a level of .27 — Eleanor was virtually pickled! When her doctor gently confronted her with the test result and suggested that Eleanor drank too much, she vehemently denied having had a drink in ten days.

During the following week, it had become apparent that Eleanor was addicted to more than alcohol. Her live-in companion called Eleanor's physician to ask what to do about Eleanor's medicine. Eleanor had prescriptions for Demerol, Codeine, and Darvon. It was no surprise to the doctors and nurses that Eleanor was agitated and sweating profusely without her drugs. She begged the hospital staff for some "real medicine."

For several days, Eleanor suffered through a difficult withdrawal. On her third day, she shrieked at the floor nurses, insisting that they let her leave the hospital. The nurses notified her physician, who convinced her to stay. On the fourth day, she announced that she was leaving. She asked a nurse to arrange for her companion to pick her up. The nurse refused, so Eleanor made her way to the phone, but she didn't have the steadiness to reach up and dial. The nurse helped her back to bed and then called me to say Eleanor wanted to leave the hospital. I contacted her physician, and he asked me to convince her to enter the hospital's chemical dependency treatment program. When I talked to Eleanor's companion, Sophie, about the problem, she was very concerned that if Eleanor went home before regaining her strength, she would die. She said Eleanor drank enormous quantities of gin, hiding the empty bottles under her bed. She also reported that Eleanor sometimes lost control of her bladder and her bowels — as well as her mind. "She's crazy when she drinks," Sophie said. "And then the next day she doesn't remember anything."

Sophie told me that Eleanor had no family or close friends. "The only person she is really friendly with is the delivery man from the liquor store."

I asked Sophie if she would help me persuade Eleanor to enter the hospital's treatment program. She agreed to come to the hospital. In the meantime, Eleanor was packing her suitcase and about to call a taxi to take her home.

Eleanor saw Sophie come out of an elevator and immediately demanded to be taken home. Sophie said, "The doctor wants to see me. Then we'll talk." Eleanor's physician, Sophie, and I met to discuss Eleanor's situation. It was clear that she was seriously ill. In fact, the doctor said she might die if she went on another extended binge. Because she was terrified of what would happen if Eleanor resumed her drinking, Sophie agreed to tell Eleanor that she wouldn't live with her until she had received treatment. The doctor said he would refuse to sign Eleanor's release form and would require her to sign a form indicating that she was leaving the hospital against medical advice.

All three of us hoped to convince Eleanor to remain in the hospital, but it seemed possible that her defenses might render her incapable of understanding our concerns. Nevertheless, Sophie, the doctor, and I agreed to attempt an intervention. I asked two elderly patients from the chemical dependency unit to introduce themselves to Eleanor and describe their treatment and recovery to her. They spent forty-five minutes with Eleanor and came away with the impression that she was a lonely woman in need of friends, but unable to recognize her dependence on chemicals.

We decided to proceed with the intervention immediately. It lasted less than fifteen minutes. Eleanor insisted that she didn't have a drinking problem. She charged Sophie with fabricating stories about her, and she threatened to sue the hospital for slander. But, she said, "I really do need a rest, and the nurses and patients seem so nice." She agreed to remain in the hospital, and she was transferred to the chemical dependency unit that afternoon.

Two days later Eleanor began to participate in educational programs and group therapy, although a week passed before she fully realized she was in a chemical dependency treatment program. She continued to be deluded about the reality of her situation for another ten days and then started to take some initial, small steps to confront her disease.

Eleanor died a year later, but it was a year of freedom from dependency on alcohol and drugs. Her funeral was attended by twenty AA friends, people with whom Eleanor had shared the experience of being straight and sober, one day at a time.

Eleanor's intervention was unusual because it did not lead to an explicit agreement to accept help for addiction. However, it succeeded in convincing Eleanor to remain in the hospital until her polluted body and mind began to recover, and she regained the capacity to make responsible choices about her life.

7
Emergency interventions

Although guided interventions usually take place only after careful preparation, there are some circumstances which call for an emergency intervention:

- When the dependent has been brought to the emergency room of a hospital as a result of an accident, overdose, or attempted suicide, especially if there is evidence to suggest that without immediate treatment the dependent might go into health-threatening withdrawal.

- When the dependent is undergoing detoxification. An intervention may be necessary to break the detoxification center's "revolving door" syndrome in which detoxification, not followed by treatment, is merely a small plateau on the virtually inevitable slide toward death.

- When the dependent has been arrested or detained by a law enforcement agency, either as a result of a legal infraction or because of a need for an emergency mental health evaluation.

- When domestic emergencies exist, especially when there is danger to any member of the family.

Under the circumstances outlined above, a helping professional is likely to be summoned by a co-dependent or the agency involved. The interventionist needs to determine the following:

- Is the person chemically dependent?

- Can an intervention team be quickly assembled even if it is comprised of only one or two people who are close to the dependent?

- Do family members or others have enough leverage to convince the dependent to accept immediate treatment?

Here is one example of an emergency intervention:

Charles, 45, was a cocaine addict whose dealer threatened him with dire consequences if money owed was not paid immediately. Charles ordered his wife to cash a savings bond. She refused, and he began beating her. Neighbors called the police who arrived to find Charles irrational and abusive. They took him to the police station and requested a consultation from a psychiatric social worker on call from the county mental health center. Charles' wife met the social worker at the police station and told her about his cocaine habit and the dealer's threat. The social worker encouraged the woman to use the crisis to persuade Charles to enter a treatment program which they had visited two months earlier during a period when Charles was remorseful. Together, his wife and the social worker talked with the police watch commander, and they came up with a plan to compel Charles to enter treatment that night. His wife told him that she loved him but could no longer live with him unless he stopped using cocaine — and that meant treatment, since the white-knuckle approach hadn't worked for him. Furthermore, she said she would pay the dealer if Charles completed treatment. The social worker told him that, based on her evaluation, she would recommend he either be delivered to treatment or to the locked ward of the county psychiatric facility. The police officer said that, since there had been no arrest, he would release him into the care of the treatment program if he followed their recommendations; otherwise the officer would order a seventy-two hour psychiatric evaluation by the proper authorities. Charles entered treatment for chemical dependency two hours later.

Emergency interventions also are carried out successfully in hospital emergency rooms. Whenever they take place, it is important that the intervention team has the necessary strength of purpose and practical leverage to act quickly.

8
For families:
Choosing an interventionist

Trained interventionists are drawn from many fields. Some are professional chemical dependency counselors; others are ministers, psychologists, health care providers, or employee assistance specialists.

For names of interventionists in your area, call the National Council on Alcoholism, your state alcohol and drug agency, and local chemical dependency treatment centers. It is extremely important to work with someone you trust, so you may want to interview several individuals before making your final selection.

The following criteria will help you find an effective interventionist:

- Your interventionist should view chemical dependency as a treatable disease characterized by certain defenses and delusions which render the dependent incapable of recovering without help. Avoid interventionists who believe chemical dependency is a moral problem or a matter of will power.

- Your interventionist should understand the necessity for including several persons in the intervention process. The dependent will find it hard to discount the data and shared concerns of several people, and therefore will be more likely to enter treatment. Also, an intervention is the beginning of healing for the entire family. Do not accept help from an interventionist who wants to intervene

103

with the dependent alone or with the dependent's spouse.

- Guided intervention, as we have said in this book, is more than a scheduled confrontation. It is a process which spans assessment and planning and continues into treatment. Choose an interventionist who understands the necessity for careful preparation. Avoid interventionists who believe they can "improvise along the way."

- Your interventionist should understand that the purpose of an intervention is not to convince the dependent to stop using alcohol or other drugs, but rather to compel the dependent into treatment.

- As a professional in the addiction field, your interventionist should be familiar with various treatment options and will be knowledgeable about AA, Al-Anon, NA, and other appropriate self-help groups. Be sure that your interventionist is not simply hunting for private clients or steering patients to a particular treatment program. Many treatment centers provide intervention services for families seeking help, but often they are willing to help you consider a variety of treatment programs.

- Finally, your interventionist should be someone who really listens to you and understands what your relationship with the dependent has been like.

Part four
From despair to decision

A concluding word

This book describes the steps which are necessary for a successful intervention, and how they have been applied in a few cases. Although this step-by-step process may appear to be relatively straightforward and easily followed, we stress that it is important to work with a counselor who is a trained interventionist.

Families and friends of alcoholics and other drug dependents should resist the urge to plan and carry out interventions on their own. Their attempts could be emotionally disastrous and will likely end in failure. However well-intentioned, family members seldom have the necessary objectivity to stay level-headed and firm in the face of the emotional conflict which is a natural part of an intervention. Families are generally too close to the dependent and too affected by the disease to be able to maintain control over the confrontation. The odds for success are far greater when an experienced interventionist is guiding the process.

What if the intervention does not produce the hoped-for result, and the dependent refuses treatment? While this is disheartening to all involved, the effort is seldom wasted. For, after interventions, dependents never again view their drinking or drug use in quite the same way. The harm the chemical use has caused in their lives has been spelled out in detail by people who are important to them. No longer are their drug problems their personal secrets, affecting only themselves. In the face of such data, a dependent will find it hard to counter with, "This is nobody's problem but mine."

The intervention has pointed the way to a specific

solution — treatment for chemical dependency — which may be accepted weeks or months later. And those who took part can find comfort in new knowledge that helps them change enabling behaviors and in the feeling that — for now — they have done all they can to effect a turnaround.

Actually, alcoholics and other drug dependents who refuse treatment after interventions are relatively few. As mentioned before, interventionists across the United States who utilize the basic approach described in this book report success rates of 80 to 90 percent. This figure represents the percentage of dependents who enter treatment immediately following the first intervention led by an appropriately trained specialist.

Interventions, when properly planned, led, and executed, can lead victims of chemical dependency and their families from despair to decision. The decision to accept treatment can be life-saving.

About the authors

Louis Krupnick and Elizabeth Krupnick are a brother and sister who grew up in a chemically dependent family. Dr. Louis Krupnick, formerly counseling supervisor at the Alcoholism Recovery Center in Palm Springs, California, is currently clinical director at Eagle Hill Treatment Center in Sandy Hook, Connecticut. He developed an outpatient treatment program in Colorado, a prevention program for youth in Massachusetts, and has been a consultant for a variety of health care and human services agencies throughout the country. Dr. Krupnick has taught hundreds of chemical dependency treatment specialists, physicians, nurses, mental health professionals, clergy, and people from industry how to incorporate guided interventions in their work. He has presented his work at major conferences across the United States.

Elizabeth Krupnick earned her master's degree from the University of Missouri School of Journalism and subsequently taught journalism to undergraduate and graduate students. Her writing includes contributions to books on special needs students and teenage pregnancy, as well as numerous articles on education, mental health and single parenting. Ms. Krupnick is currently a public relations professional working in Hartford, Connecticut.

The Twelve Steps*

1. We admitted we were powerless over alcohol — that our lives had become unmanageable.
2. Came to believe that a Power greater than ourselves could restore us to sanity.
3. Made a decision to turn our will and our lives over to the care of God, as we understood Him.
4. Made a searching and fearless moral inventory of ourselves.
5. Admitted to God, to ourselves and to another human being the exact nature of our wrongs.
6. Were entirely ready to have God remove all these defects of character.
7. Humbly asked Him to remove our shortcomings.
8. Made a list of all persons we had harmed, and became willing to make amends to them all.
9. Made direct amends to such people wherever possible, except when to do so would injure them or others.
10. Continued to take personal inventory and when we were wrong, promptly admitted it.
11. Sought through prayer and meditation to improve our conscious contact with God, as we understood Him, praying only for knowledge of His will for us and the power to carry that out.
12. Having had a spiritual awakening as the result of these steps, we tried to carry this message to alcoholics and to practice these principles in all our affairs.

*The Twelve Steps reprinted by permission of AA World Services, Inc.©1939, 1955, and 1976.

Am I an alcoholic/drug dependent?

1. Do I lose time from work due to drinking/using?
2. Is drinking/using making my home life unhappy?
3. Do I drink/use drugs because I am shy with other people?
4. Is drinking/using affecting my reputation?
5. Have I ever felt remorse after drinking/using?
6. Have I gotten into financial difficulties as a result of drinking/using?
7. Do I turn to lower companions and an inferior environment when drinking/using?
8. Does my drinking/drug use make me careless of my family's welfare?
9. Has my ambition decreased since drinking/using?
10. Do I crave a drink/drug at a definite time daily?
11. Do I want a drink/drug the next morning?
12. Does drinking/drug use cause me to have difficulty in sleeping?
13. Has my efficiency decreased since drinking/using?
14. Is drinking/drug use jeopardizing my job or business?
15. Do I drink/use to escape from worries or troubles?
16. Do I drink/use drugs alone?
17. Have I ever had a complete loss of memory as a result of drinking/using?
18. Has my physician ever treated me for drinking/drug use?
19. Do I drink/use to build up my self-confidence?
20. Have I ever been to a hospital or institution on account of my drinking/drug use?

The above test questions were adapted from those used by Johns Hopkins University Hospital, Baltimore, Maryland.

Am I affected by the alcohol/drug use of someone close to me?

1. Do I worry a lot about or lose sleep over someone's drinking?
2. Do I cover up for someone else's drinking behavior — making excuses or telling lies when the drinker is irresponsible, misses work because of a hangover (do I call it "the flu"?), or forgets commitments?
3. Do I play sleuth — searching for telltale paraphernalia or bottles, reading mail, listening in on phone conversations?
4. Do I hide, empty out, or throw away bottles?
5. Do I make threats — like "If you don't stop drinking, I'll leave home" — and then never carry them out? Or wrench promises from the drinker/user that I know will not be kept?
6. Do I blame the drinker's (drug user's) behavior on other people or situations — an unhappy childhood, rejection, the "wrong" kind of friends, military service, frustration in a job?
7. Do I sometimes feel guilty or responsible for the person's alcohol or drug use?
8. Do I begin to withdraw from friends and activities outside the home because of someone's alcohol or drug use?
9. Do I find that I am subject to swinging moods — ranging from loneliness, to hurt, anger, fear, guilt, or depression — because of another person's drinking or drug use?
10. Have I taken on responsibilities or debts that used to be handled by the drinker/drug-user?

11. Is my relationship — especially if it is an intimate one — affected by feelings of revulsion?
12. Am I walking an emotional tightrope, trying to cover my inner turmoil with outer calm, to keep from upsetting the user/drinker and sending her/him into a binge?
13. Do I dread trips or holidays or even an evening out because of what the person may do if he/she drinks too much?
14. Do I feel that if the drinker only loved me enough she/he would stop drinking?
15. If the drinker is my spouse and we have children, are they showing signs of reacting to the situation too — by becoming withdrawn or rebellious, becoming sexually promiscuous or getting into drugs or alcohol? Do the children sometimes take sides either with the drinker or with me?
16. Have I suffered physically as a result of the stress in my household? Muscle tension, shakiness, nausea, stomach cramps, high blood pressure, rashes, headaches, eating too much or almost nothing.
17. Do I take out my frustrations on others around me, my children, friends, associates, pets, and then feel guilty afterwards?
18. Are there increasing arguments over money, responsibilities, drinking or using behavior?
19. Do I feel that if the drinking or using would stop everything would be all right?
20. Am I feeling helpless, hopeless, defeated, just plain exhausted?

From *Please Don't Do Nothing* by Pat Meyer, Jane Thomas Noland, and Gary Swedberg.
©City of Wayzata (Minnesota), 1984.
Used by permission.

If you have answered YES to one or more questions on either questionnaire, you may want to see a professional who understands chemical dependency.

Bibliography

Ablon, J. Family structure and behavior in alcoholism: a review of the literature. In B. Kissin and H. Begleiter (Eds.), *The Biology of Alcoholism.* Vol. 4. New York: Plenum, 1976.

Alateen: Hope for the Children of Alcoholics. New York: Al-Anon Family Group Headquarters, 1973.

Alcoholics Anonymous (3rd Ed.). New York: Alcoholics Anonymous World Services, 1976.

Alibrandi, T. *Young Alcoholics.* Minneapolis: CompCare Publications, 1978.

Berenson, D. Alcohol and the family system. In P. J. Guerin, Jr. (Ed.), *Family Therapy: Theory and Practice.* New York: Gardner Press, 1976.

Berne, E. *Games People Play.* New York: Grove Press, 1964.

Black, C. *It Will Never Happen to Me.* Newport Beach, CA: ACT, 1981.

Black, C. *My Dad Loves Me/My Dad Has A Disease.* Newport Beach, CA: ACT, 1979.

Bowe, M. Alcoholism as viewed through family systems theory and family psychotherapy. *Annals of the New York Academy of Sciences,* 1974, 233, 115-122.

Brandon, D. *Zen in the Art of Helping.* New York: Delta, 1976.

Brooks, K. *The Secret Everybody Knows.* San Diego: Kroc Foundation, 1981.

Brown, S., and Yalom, I. D. Interactional group therapy with alcoholics. *Journal of Studies on Alcohol,* 199. 38, 426-456.

Carnes, P. *The Sexual Addiction.* Minneapolis: CompCare Publications, 1983.

Chafetz, M. E., Blane, H. T., and Hill, M. J. Children of alcoholics: Observations in a child guidance clinic. *Quarterly Journal of Studies on Alcohol,* 1971. 32, 687-698.

Cork, M. R. *The Forgotten Children.* Toronto: Addiction Research Foundation, 1971.

Delin, B. *The Sex Offender.* Boston: Beacon Press, 1978.

Diagnostic and Statistical Manual of Mental Disorders (3rd Ed.). Washington: American Psychiatric Association, 1980.

Dilemma of the Alcoholic Marriage. New York: Al-Anon Family Group Headquarters, 1971.

Donlan, J. *I Never Saw the Sun Rise.* Minneapolis: Comp-Care Publications, 1977.

Edwards, P., Harvey, C., and Whitehead, P. C. Wives of alcoholics: A critical review and analysis. *Quarterly Journal of Studies on Alcohol,* 1973, 34, 112.

Ellis, A. *Reason and Emotion in Psychotherapy.* New York: Lyle Stuart, 1962.

Ellis, A., and Harper, R. A. *A New Guide to Rational Living.* Hollywood: Wilshire Book Company, 1976.

Erickson, Doug. *Please Uncover What My Chemical Use is Hiding*. Available from Doug Erickson, 5020 Richmond Drive, Minneapolis, MN 55436.

Estes, N. J., and Hanson, K. J. (Eds.), *Alcoholism: Development, Consequences, and Interventions*. St. Louis: C.V. Mosby, 1977.

Ewing, J. A., and Fox, R. E. Family therapy of alcoholism. In J. Masserman (Ed.), *Current Psychiatric Therapies*. Vol. 8. New York: Grune and Stratton, 1968.

Fox, R. Group psychotherapy with alcoholics. *International Journal of Group Psychotherapy*, 1961, 12, 56-63.

Fox, R. Modifications of group psychotherapy for alcoholics. *American Journal of Orthopsychiatry*, 1965, 35, 258-259.

Haley, J. *Problem-Solving Therapy*. San Francisco: Jossey-Bass, 1976.

Hayman, M. Current attitudes to alcoholism of psychiatrists in Southern California. *American Journal of Psychiatry* 127:7, 1971.

Heilman, R. O. *Dynamics of Drug Dependency*. Center City, MN: Hazelden, 1973.

Holmstrom, L., and Burgess, A. *The Victim of Rape: Institutional Reactions*. New York: John Wiley and Sons, 1978.

Howard, D., and Howard, N. *A Family Approach to Problem Drinking*. Columbia, MO: Family Training Center, 1976.

Howard, D., and Howard, N. *The Family Counseling Model - An Early Intervention of Problem Drinking*. Columbia, MO: Family Training Center, 1977.

Hubbell, J. A dynamic new approach to the alcoholic. *Readers Digest*, May, 1976.

Jackson, J. The adjustments of the family to the crisis of alcoholism. *Quarterly Journal of Studies on Alcohol* 15, 1954, 562-586.

James, J. E., and Golman, M. Behavior trend of wives of alcoholics. *Quarterly Journal of Studies on Alcohol* 32, 1971, 373-381.

Jellinek, E. M. *Disease Concept of Alcoholism*. New Haven: United Printing Services, 1960.

Johnson, V. *I'll Quit Tomorrow*. New York: Harper and Row, 1980.

Justice, B., and Justice, R. *The Broken Taboo: Sex in the Family*. New York: Human Science Press, 1979.

Kellerman, J. L. *Alcoholism: A Merry-Go-Round Named Denial*. Al-Anon Family Group Headquarters, 1969.

Madsen, W. The American Alcoholic: *The Nature-Nurture Controversy in Alcoholic Research and Therapy*. Springfield: Charles C. Thomas, 1974.

Mann, M. *Marty Mann Answers Your Questions about Drinking and Alcoholism*. New York: Holt, Rinehart and Winston, 1970.

Maxwell, R. *The Booze Battle.* New York: Praeger, 1976.

Mills, P. *Rape Intervention Resource Manual.* Springfield, IL: Charles C. Thomas, 1977.

Minuchin, S. Family therapy: technique or theory: In J. Masserman (Ed.), *Science and Psychoanalysis.* Vol. 14. New York: Grune and Stratton, 1969.

Nero, J. *If Only My Wife Could Drink Like a Lady.* Minneapolis: CompCare Publications, 1977.

Ohliger, P. No pills to alcoholics. Orange County, CA: Medical Association *Bulletin,* Feb. 1974.

Rae, J. B., and Drewery, J. Interpersonal patterns in alcoholic marriages. *British Journal of Psychiatry.* 1972, 120, 615, 621.

Rogers, C. *Client-Centered Therapy.* Boston: Houghton Mifflin, 1951.

Royce, James E. *Alcohol Problems and Alcoholism: A Comprehensive Survey.* New York: The Free Press, 1981.

Satir, V. *Peoplemaking.* Palo Alto: Science and Behavior Books, 1972.

Scott, L. *The Intervention Guide.* Available from Linda Scott, Alcoholism Recovery Center, Desert Hospital, Palm Springs, CA.

Shulman, G., and O'Connor, R. The rehabilitation of the alcoholic. In Gitlow, S., and Peyser, H., *Alcoholism: A Practical Treatment Guide.* New York: Grune and Stratton, 1980.

Small, J. *Becoming Naturally Therapeutic* (Revised ed.). Austin: The Eupsychian Press, 1981.

Small, J. *Transformers: The Therapists of the Future.* Hollywood, FL: Health Communications, 1982.

Steiner, C. *Games Alcoholics Play.* New York: Grove Press, 1971.

Steinglass, P. Experimenting with family treatment approaches to alcoholism, 1950-1975, a review. *Family Process,* 1976, 15, 97-123.

Swift, H. A., and Williams, T. *Recovery for the Whole Family.* Center City, MN: Hazelden, 1975.

Tiebout, H. M. *Surrender Versus Compliance in Therapy with Special Reference to Alcoholism.* Greenwich, CT: National Council on Alcoholism, 1952.

Tiebout, H. M. The ego factor in surrender in alcoholism. *Quarterly Journal of Studies on Alcohol,* 1954, 15, 610-621.

Tiebout, H. M. Intervention in psychotherapy. *The American Journal of Psychoanalysis,* 1962, 22, 1-6.

Ward, R. F., and Faillace, L. A. The alcoholic and his helpers. *Quarterly Journal of Studies on Alcohol,* 1970, 31, 684-691.

Wegscheider, D. *If Only My Family Understood Me.* Minneapolis: CompCare Publications, 1979.

Wegscheider, S. *Another Chance.* Palo Alto: Science and Behavior Books, 1981.

Weinberg, J. R. *Why do alcoholics deny their problem?* Minneapolis: CompCare Publications, 1977.

Zink, M. *Ways to Live More Comfortably with Your Alcoholic.* Minneapolis: CompCare Publications, 1977.

Guides to recovery
from CompCare Publications

Alcohol and Drugs and You and Me, Vern Drilling. Basic, non-threatening information about harmful involvement with alcohol and other drugs: how to recognize it, how to get help. An employee assistance tool for business and other organizations to distribute to employees at all levels. Pamphlet.

The All-American Cocaine Story, David Britt (a pseudonym). A young executive's personal struggle to overcome addiction to what some doctors call "the most seductive drug of all" — cocaine. A readable, realistic assessment of an epidemic problem in the United States today. Trade paperback.

... But I Didn't Make Any Noise About It, Cindy Lewis-Steere. The story of her teenage son's drug dependency. A moving account of a family's crisis and painful growth illustrates clearly that, as the entire family is affected by one member's drug problem, all members are involved in the recovery process. Recommended by counselors for use in parent and family groups, as well as by individual families. Pamphlet.

Consider the Alternative, Lee M. Silverstein. A caring counselor and nationally known lecturer at alcoholism and health conferences has synthesized popular theories about therapy into a personal guide for living. Greeted with enthusiasm by Albert Ellis, Sidney B. Simon (who wrote the foreword), Joel Fort, William Glasser, John Powell, and many other experts. Trade paperback.

A Day At A Time. Now with 400,000 in print, this pocket-sized book of daily messages offers confidence, strength, resolve, hope, and serenity. Especially helpful to those in Twelve Step programs. Hardcover.

Going Home, A Re-entry Guide for the Newly Sober, Janet Geringer Woititz, Ed.D. A compassionate, straight-talking guide for anyone who is newly sober, whether sobriety began in a residential or outpatient program or through AA alone. Examines predicaments, issues, special problems and hurdles faced when a person begins a chemical-free life. By a college professor, alcoholism counselor, and author of *Marriage on the Rocks* and *Adult Children of Alcoholics.* Pamphlet.

I Never Saw the Sun Rise, Joan Donlan. A high school counselor says: "This book should be required reading for every high school student in the country — and for all parents." A true, as-it-happened journal by a talented 15-year-old tells of her dependency on drugs and alcohol, her treatment, her recovery. Important insights for teens and adults. Trade paperback.

If Only My Family Understood Me ... Don Wegscheider, foreword by Virginia Satir. A family can find new balance through stress. The same insights which help troubled families can help any family (troubled or not) have more fun living together. A "whole person" approach, particularly useful for alcoholic families and their counselors. Trade paperback.

If Only My Wife Could Drink Like a Lady, Jack Nero. Intimate, heartening story of a one-in-ten marriage to survive a wife's alcoholism — by her "mirror alcoholic" husband. Essential information about AA and Al-Anon for alcoholics and those close to them. "May save some lives and ease the tension for families of alcoholics." *Jan Frazer Book Review.* Trade paperback.

The Sexual Addiction, Patrick Carnes, Ph.D. The first book to recognize "the disease of the '80s": compulsive sexual behavior, what it is and what can be done to recover from it. Hardcover/trade paperback.

The Twelve Steps for Everyone ... Who Really Wants Them. Keys to spiritual health and emotional wealth based on the Twelve Step path developed by AA. Clearly interpreted by members of EHA (Emotional Health Anonymous). Trade paperback.

The Winner's Way, Carol Hegarty. Step by Step, the newcomer is introduced to the Twelve Steps of AA. These all-important, effective concepts are offered in words anyone can understand and relate to. Answers basic questions about the Steps; includes glossary. Pamphlet.

Young Alcoholics, Tom Alibrandi. An alcoholism counselor takes a hard look at teenage drinking. "Offers young problem drinkers (and parents who want to help them) practical, proven series of approaches to recovery." *Los Angeles Times.* Trade paperback.

Young Winners' Way, Dennis Nelson and Jane Thomas Noland. The first interpretation of the Twelve Steps of AA for recovering teenaged alcoholics and drug-dependents — by a counselor and a parent, with recovering young people's own stories. Pamphlet.